S0-AUJ-501

Early Socialisation

Early Socialisation looks at how individuals come to be who they are. It deals with the way in which early childhood experiences shape a person's psychological nature through the processes of sociability and attachment and shows how these processes relate to emotional and cognitive development. Topics covered include: bonding, attachment, deprivation, separation and privation, as well as enrichment. Social and cultural variations are considered and theories of attachment and loss are described and evaluated.

This highly accessible text is written specifically for the student new to psychology. It provides clear, up-to-date explanations of all the important concepts in this area of human development and both theory and empirical research are carefully described and assessed.

Cara Flanagan is an experienced author and Assessor and Team Leader for AEB A-level psychology. Her most recent books include *Practicals for psychology* (Routledge 1998), *Psychology A-level study guide* (1994) and *Applying psychology to early childhood development* (1996). She is a co-editor for the series with Kevin Silber.

Routledge Modular Psychology

Series editors: Cara Flanagan is the Assessor for the Associated Examining Board (AEB) and an experienced A-level author. Kevin Silber is Senior Lecturer in Psychology at Staffordshire University. Both are A-level examiners in the U

The *Routledge Modular Psychology* series is a completely new approach to introductory level psychology, tailor-made to the new modular style of teaching. Each short book covers a topic in more detail than any large textbook can, allowing teacher and student to select material exactly to suit any particular course or project.

The books have been written especially for those students new to higher-level study, whether at school, college or university. They include specially designed features to help with technique, such as a model essay at an average level with an examiner's comments to show how extra marks can be gained. The authors are all examiners and teachers at the introductory level.

The *Routledge Modular Psychology* texts are all user-friendly and accessible and include the following features:

- practice essays with specialist commentary to show how to achieve a higher grade
- chapter summaries to assist with revision
- progress and review exercises
- glossary of key terms
- summaries of key research
- further reading to stimulate ongoing study and research
- website addresses for additional information
- cross-referencing to other books in the series

Also available in this series (titles listed by syllabus section):

ATYPICAL DEVELOPMENT AND ABNORMAL BEHAVIOUR

Psychopathology
John D. Stirling and Jonathan S. E. Hellewell

Therapeutic Approaches in Psychology
Susan Cave

BIO-PSYCHOLOGY

Cortical Functions
John Stirling

The Physiological Basis of Behaviour: Neural and hormonal processes
Kevin Silber

Awareness: Biorhythms, sleep and dreaming
Evie Bentley

COGNITIVE PSYCHOLOGY

Memory and Forgetting
John Henderson

Perception: Theory, development and organisation
Paul Rookes and Jane Willson (forthcoming)

COMPARATIVE PSYCHOLOGY

Reproductive Strategies
John Gammon (forthcoming)

DEVELOPMENTAL PSYCHOLOGY

Cognitive Development
David Cohen (forthcoming)

Early Socialisation: Sociability and attachment
Cara Flanagan

PERSPECTIVES AND RESEARCH

Conceptual Issues and Debates
Andy Bell (forthcoming)

Controversies in Psychology
Philip Banyard

Ethical Issues in Psychology
Mike Cardwell (forthcoming)

Introducing Research and Data in Psychology: A guide to methods and analysis
Ann Searle

SOCIAL PSYCHOLOGY

Social Influences
Kevin Wren

Interpersonal Relationships
Diana Dwyer (forthcoming)

STUDY GUIDE

Exam Success in AEB Psychology
Paul Humphreys

OTHER TITLES

Health Psychology
Anthony Curtis (forthcoming)

Sport Psychology
Marr Jarvis

Lethbridge Community College Library

Early Socialisation
Sociability and attachment

Cara Flanagan

London and New York

First published
1999 by Routledge
11 New Fetter Lane, London EC4P 4EE

Simultaneously published in the USA and Canada
by Routledge
29 West 35th Street, New York, NY 10001

Routledge Ltd is a Taylor & Francis Group Company

© 1999 Cara Flanagan

Typeset in Times by Routledge
Printed and bound in Great Britain by St Edmundsbury – St Edmundsbury, Suffolk

All rights reserved. No part of this book may be reprinted or
reproduced or utilised in any form or by any electronic,
mechanical, or other means, now known or hereafter
invented, including photocopying and recording, or in any
information storage or retrieval system, without permission
in writing from the publishers.

British Library Cataloguing in Publication Data
A catalogue record for this book is available from the British Library

Library of Congress Cataloging in Publication Data
Early socialisation: sociability and attachment/Cara Flanagan.
Includes bibliographical references and index.
1. Socialization. 2. Child development. 3. Child psychology.
I. Title. II. Title: Early socialization. III. Series.
HQ783.F53 1999
99–12739
303.32–dc21
CIP

ISBN 0–415–18656–0 (hbk)
ISBN 0–415–18657–9 (pbk)

To my mother, Geraldine, to whom I am profoundly attached!

Contents

Illustrations

Acknowledgements

The series editors and Routledge acknowledge the expert help of Paul Humphreys, Examiners and Reviser for A-level psychology, in compiling the Study aids chapter of each book in this series.

They also acknowledge the Associated Examining Board (AEB) for granting permission to use their examination material. The AEB do not accept responsibility for the answers or examiner comment in the Study aids chapter of this book or any other book in the series.

Thanks also to the following published for permission to reproduce the drawings in Figure 3.1 from Konrad Lorenz *King Solomon's Ring* © 1983 Deutscher Taschenbuch Verlag, Munich/Germany. © for the English translation: Marjorie Kerr Wilson, Altenberg/Austria.

The author would also like to thank Geraldine Lux Flanagan for the considerable advice and appreciation offered during the writing of this book, her family (Rob, Pip, Jack and Rosie) for their enduring support, Moira Taylor at Routledge for her consistent good humour and Kevin Silber for doing it with me.

Introduction

Some early views of childhood
This century
Summary

The focus of this book is on how you came to be who you are. It deals with the way in which early childhood experiences shape a person's psychological nature. A key part of your personality is your emotional self, and this aspect of self has a critical influence on all other aspects of development. An unhappy child finds it difficult to focus on learning because emotional tension interferes with his/her ability to process information systematically. An insecure child doesn't want to wander away from the home environment and explore the world. Therefore, one of the first 'tasks' for the infant is to find an emotional starting place, a **secure base**, and to begin his or her emotional development.

The infant's early social experiences are the means by which it develops emotionally. Infants are generally sociable – they like people and want to interact with them. Some of these social relationships are special. That is to say, people form special bonds with certain others. For example, the infant is likely to form a special bond or **attachment** with its **caregiver**(s). Attachments provide security and this enables the infant to explore the world around him or her.

The study of early **sociability** and attachment is not carried out just for understanding the developmental process. It also enables us to advise people who care for young children about how to improve early experiences.

Some early views of childhood

The attitudes that we, in Britain, hold about how young children should be treated have changed remarkably in the last 100 years. Consider the following advice given to parents in a book on childcare, 'Never hug and kiss [your children], never let them sit on your lap. If you must, kiss them on the forehead when they say goodnight' (Watson, 1928). Such advice would not appear today.

Our attitudes are the product of our history and our **culture**. In the ancient past, children were treated very differently in this country and elsewhere. For instance, to take an extreme example, in Sparta around the ninth century boys aged 7 were removed from their homes and raised in public barracks. This undoubtedly was an important factor in turning them into the warriors who were vital to the Spartan nation. So we can see that childrearing methods were, and are, related to a culture's view of what is desirable in adulthood.

Philosophers of the seventeenth and eighteenth centuries helped to change Western views of childhood. One 'school' of thought was that children are born inherently selfish and their base instincts had to be controlled by society. In other words, they had to be socialised into caring adults. In contrast, Jean Jacques Rousseau, a French philosopher, claimed that we are born with an innate sense of right and wrong. We should respect the inherent goodness of children and give them the freedom to develop naturally. Each of these views had important effects on the way children were, and continue to be, treated and educated.

The beginnings of childhood

Throughout history adults have recognised childhood as a distinct and important period of development. In fact until recently it was regarded as the only period of development! More recently psychologist have begun to talk about 'lifespan development' and to describe how adults continue to 'grow', psychologically speaking. This book, however, will focus mainly on emotional development during childhood.

In the past, children were generally expected to take on many adult responsibilities. They went to work and/or helped at home. Very few were educated or, if they were, this was an outside-of-hours activity. Compulsory schooling first appeared as recently as the second half of the nineteenth century. Around the same time the first case of child abuse was brought to court, signalling a recognition that children were not simply their parents' possessions but individuals with their own rights. The actual case concerned a child called Mary Ellen, who lived in New York. Her neighbours objected to the way she was being treated by her parents and used the only laws available at the time – which protected animals from abuse – to argue that the child was a member of the animal kingdom and deserved the court's protection as much as any non-human animal.

This century

The next phase in our changing views was to look at the effects that deprivation might have on the developing child, particularly in terms of emotional development. Freud had introduced the idea that early experiences may well have lasting consequences especially in terms of adult maladjustment.

The maternal deprivation hypothesis

Around the time of the Second World War a variety of psychologists published research about the effects of separation and **deprivation** – could it be that early separation between parents and children leads to lasting emotional disturbance? Spitz and Wolf (1946) studied 100 infants who had been separated from their mothers, and found that the infants did become severely depressed. Skeels and Dye (1939) and later Skodak and Skeels (1945, 1949) observed the negative effects of emotional deprivation. They found that children in orphanages suffered impaired intellectual development but that this could be avoided if they were given increased adult attention, by being moved from the orphanage to a home for mentally retarded adults. In other words, these studies showed that children will suffer lasting consequences if deprived of care and attention during their early years.

Spitz and Wolf used the term **anaclitic depression** to describe the maladjustment associated with prolonged separation. Bowlby called it **affectionless psychopathy**, a lack of ability to experience affection or emotion. John Bowlby was the author of the most influential theories of the effects of emotional deprivation (the **maternal deprivation** hypothesis and his **attachment theory**). He conducted his own research (Bowlby, 1946) using data collected in a Child Guidance Clinic. He found that those children who experienced early and prolonged separations from their caregiver were more likely to become delinquents (lacking empathy for others) whereas other child patients, who had not experienced early separations, were 'just' emotionally disturbed rather than being without emotion (affectionless).

These were revolutionary concepts at the time. They suggested that **maternal deprivation** was a cause of mental illness and cognitive impairment. In 1953, the World Health Organisation commissioned John Bowlby to write a report, which was entitled *Maternal care and child health*. He subsequently summed his hypothesis up in a famous quote: 'prolonged deprivation of a young child of maternal care may have grave and far reaching effects on his character ... similar in form ... to deprivation of vitamin(s) in infancy' (Bowlby, 1953).

Evaluation

Some people might say that these studies were conducted a long time ago and the methodology used is open to question. For example, we cannot be sure that all of the observed ill-effects were due to separations or that institutional effects were due to psychological rather than physical deprivation.

Another way to assess the value of this research is to consider the positive effects it had. First of all, Bowlby's theory has generated a considerable body of empirical work, such as studies by Mary Ainsworth (who originally worked with Bowlby), and a longitudinal study of Scottish infants by Schaffer and Emerson (which contributed to later modifications of Bowlby's theory). This research is examined in later chapters of this book.

Bowlby's work also had important political effects. He said that bad homes were better than good institutions and felt that some case workers 'live in the sentimental glamour of saving neglected children from wicked parents' (Bowlby *et al.*, 1952). Such sentiments helped turn the tide against institutional care for children.

Bowlby's work was also used to argue that the absence of mothers led to disturbed children, a point which had important implications for child care. If mothers must be present to ensure the happiness of their children then mothers should stay at home and not work. Such a policy may well have suited the government of the day because women had worked during the war but now men needed their jobs and this was a way to get women to stay at home. Some psychologists, such as Rodman (1987), felt quite cynical about this and warned Bowlby that his views were being misused by politicians.

Imprinting and bonding

Research using non-human animals was fundamental in the later development of Bowlby's theory. Two key figures are Konrad Lorenz, an ethologist who studied geese, and Harry Harlow who studied rhesus monkeys.

Lorenz suggested that goslings were innately programmed to **imprint** on the first moving object they saw on hatching. This imprint (or lasting impression) created a bond between hatchling and caregiver which was important for survival and future reproduction. It occurs most easily in a **sensitive period** after hatching.

Harlow's work demonstrated that infant monkeys who were deprived of *interactive* physical contact suffered severe permanent consequences such as being unable to form successful reproductive relationships in adulthood. The image of Harlow's isolated, frightened monkeys clinging to cloth-covered models conveys a powerful message about the need for early bonding. (See Figure 3.2 on p. 32.)

Imprinting, bonding and attachment

The distinctions between imprinting, **bonding** and attachment are not easy to make and sometimes the terms are used rather interchangeably. Reber (1995) defines bonding as:

> The forming of a relationship ... specifically between the mother and her newborn. Some use the term as a synonym for attachment; others distinguish it as a separate process that occurs during the first few hours after the birth of the infant.

Reber defines attachment as 'an emotional tie'. Harlow talks about both bonding and attachment bonds in relation to his work on monkeys. Imprinting is generally accepted to be a specialised form of learning which takes place rapidly during early development but

> whether or not mammals show imprinting is contentious. Lambs and young goats (kids) appear to imprint, and Bowlby's theory of attachment in human young certainly drew heavily on ideas from imprinting theory and research.

(Cardwell, 1996)

My suggestion is to use the term imprinting when considering **precocial** animals, that is those animals who are mobile from birth such as geese; to use the term 'bonding' to describe some non-human animal relationships or the tie between very young infants and their caregivers; and to reserve the term 'attachment' for the emotional bonds which develop rather more slowly in higher mammals and older infants.

Each of these concepts (imprinting, bonding and attachment) will be discussed in separate chapters of this book.

Bowlby's theory of attachment

Bowlby's original theory was one of maternal deprivation, influenced by his training in Freudian **psychoanalysis**. It has been suggested that there are parallels between Bowlby's concept of maternal deprivation and Freud's concept of oral deprivation; both lead to predictable negative outcomes in adulthood.

In the light of empirical research on imprinting and bonding described above, Bowlby reshaped his theory into one with a more ethological perspective. The key characteristic of ethology is a focus on observing the *whole* organism in the context of its interaction with other animals and its environment. It is a science of observation and an analysis of the *function* of particular behaviours. Ethologists look at the effects of behaviours, in particular at the extent to which the behaviour makes the individual and species better *adapted* to its environment. **Adaptiveness** is an evolutionary concept which describes behaviour in terms of its survival value and states that any behaviour which increases survival (and future reproduction) is adaptive. The implications of this concept are that we are more likely to observe adaptive behaviours than non-adaptive ones. This is because individuals who have the latter characteristics are less likely to reproduce and so their characteristics die out!

In this book I have dealt with the theory of attachment by looking at the empirical evidence first, in Chapters 3 to 6, and then reviewing and assessing the whole theory in the light of this evidence.

Sociability

Before even looking at the evidence related to deprivation and attachment, we need to consider sociability. You may ask 'Why'? Bowlby argued that attachment is adaptive and **innate**. The basis of this innate predisposition is found in the infant's 'pre-programming' to respond to social situations and to elicit caregiving. Adults are similarly 'programmed' to respond. These innate behaviours, or innate **sociability**, lead to the formation of mutual attachments which maintain proximity and promote survival. The next chapter looks at research on sociability.

Cross-cultural research

We began this first chapter by looking at how attitudes towards children have varied over time and culture. Our concept that attachment is vital to healthy development is not shared by all cultures. There have been many studies looking at attachment and emotional development in other cultures, and these are discussed in Chapter 7. Such research gives us a perspective on the universal nature of the effects of deprivation and attachment.

Summary

The aim of this chapter was to outline our changing attitudes towards emotional development in childhood and to provide a framework for the rest of this book. Attitudes towards childhood differ historically and culturally. These differences are due to changes in attitudes and philosophical orientations as well as empirical research. Central influences have come from research with deprived children in the 1940s, which led John Bowlby to develop a theory of maternal deprivation. Other influences came from the research by Lorenz and Harlow on imprinting and bonding, which helped Bowlby to further his theory of attachment. The later version emphasised how innate social behaviours (sociability) led to the formation of reciprocal attachments which were highly adaptive. There are key distinctions to be made between imprinting, bonding and attachment, as well as deprivation and privation.

Further reading

Berryman, J.C., Hargreaves, D., Herbert, M. and Taylor, A. (1994) *Developmental psychology and you*. Leicester: BPS Books. An accessible introductory textbook for developmental psychology, including chapters on early relationships and influences.

Schaffer, H.R. (1995) *Early socialisation*. Leicester: BPS Books. Part of a series of Open Learning Units designed to give short introductions to key areas in psychology. Clearly written though lacking in depth because it's a short book (45 pages).

—— (1996) *Social development*. Oxford: Blackwell. A textbook by the same author which contains material relevant to the whole of this book.

2

Sociability

Introduction

Sociability is the tendency to seek the company of others, to be friendly. Some people are more sociable than others but pretty much everyone shows some signs of sociability. Babies love interactions with people, animals and things. Our central interest in this book is the importance that these interactions have in the formation of emotional relationships. An infant who elicits and responds to social interactions is more likely to form such relationships. An unsociable baby will form fewer attachments. The infant's sociability is determined by both nature and nurture.

Innate social abilities

Social abilities are those behaviours which enable and encourage social interactions. A baby who leads adults to feel interest and affection has a greater chance of survival. This is because the adult is encouraged to remain close to protect the infant and provide food. It also means that the infant maximises his or her learning opportunities by having adults to interact with. This is an **evolutionary explanation** of sociability because it accounts for behaviour in terms of its adaptiveness and survival value. Being sociable means it is more likely that the infant will survive, and of course only those infants who survive can go on to reproduce, and those individuals who reproduce create offspring who are likely to inherit the same behaviours, and so on!

Adults are also likely to be innately 'programmed' to respond to signals from babies. Caregivers who don't do this will decrease their infant's chance of survival. The infants who are more likely to survive are those whose parents have 'caregiving **genes**' (genes are the units of inheritance).

Therefore we find the survivors are likely to be those individuals who, as babies, innately produced infant–caregiver social signals and who, as adults, responded to them.

Specific behaviours

Some examples of behaviours in the infant's repertoire are listed below:

- *A 'baby face'*. All young animals have an appearance which makes them appealing: a large forehead, large round eyes, and soft, rounded features (Lorenz, 1943; see Figure 2.1). Such faces are rather similar to the Teletubbies or even Barbie! It is no accident that toy manufacturers have used these features to appeal to their consumers. Alley (1981) found that adults judged drawings of infant faces to be more adorable than those of a 4-year-old. Incidentally, you might wonder about whether the way an infant looks would count as a 'behaviour'; in the broadest sense of the word it is.

Figure 2.1 Infants of many species display what Lorenz called the 'kewpie-doll' effect that makes them appear lovable and elicits caregiving

Source: After Shaffer, 1993, in Lorenz, 1943

- *Smiling*. When someone smiles at you, it makes you feel they like you. It is a non-verbal signal which makes people come back for more. There is some debate about how old infants are before they begin to smile. Very young infants may smile because they feel pleasure. The first social smiles (smiling at someone) probably occur around 8 weeks but it is hard to distinguish asocial from social smiles. How do we know? It's as well to remember that all research with infants is very prone to be influenced by the researchers' expectations.

- *Cooing* is a vocal signal which communicates pleasure and adults respond with interest.

- *Crying*. Most people feel uncomfortable when they hear an infant, or an adult, crying. This is no accident because it helps to ensure that someone will respond. Some adults suggest that an infant who is crying is somehow being 'very clever' and 'manipulating you'. But it is a mechanism which has evolved exactly because it does just that, and thus maximises survival by keeping the caregiver(s) close. Not every society believes that children should learn to be alone but Western society seems to feel that crying should be limited. Therefore a crying infant may have a counterproductive effect, as in cases of child abuse where parents are driven to their wits' end by a child who won't stop crying.

- *Imitation*. 'Imitation is the sincerest form of flattery' and also a means of communicating liking. You might have noticed that if you stick your tongue out to a young baby, the baby will respond by doing the same. Meltzoff and Moore have conducted many studies of infant imitation (1977, 1983, 1989, 1992) and found that babies of less than 7 days old were also able to imitate other face movements, such as furrowing their foreheads or opening their mouth. This ability demonstrates that right from the beginning the infant is *participating* in a social exchange. One important feature of this to note is that the infant can't know what it is doing yet is able to translate what it sees into a matching movement of its own facial muscles (see Figure 2.2).

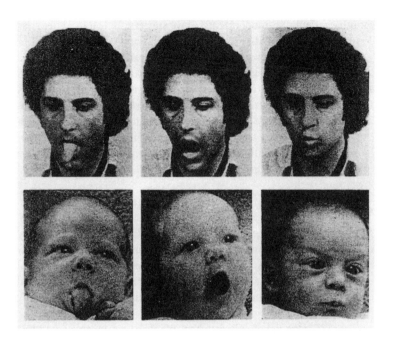

Figure 2.2 Photographs showing infants imitating adult expressions

Source: Meltzoff and Moore, 1977

Emotional expression

The infant clearly has a large repertoire of behaviours which enable it to attract and maintain the attention of caregivers. Perhaps one of the most important behaviours is emotional expression, which underlies all the other abilities mentioned above.

Johnson *et al.* (1982) interviewed mothers who reported that their 1-month-old babies displayed at least five distinct emotions: interest, joy and surprise as well as anger and fear. Izard *et al.* (1980) also found evidence that very young infants reliably expressed emotion. Izard *et al.* established this by taking photographs of infants expressing an emotional response: they might have been given an ice cube to hold or their mother had just left the room. Other adults were asked to label the emotion displayed in the baby's face. Infants of 2 months reliably showed interest, joy, surprise, anger and fear, as Johnson *et al.* reported.

Such emotions have been described as **primary emotions**. Izard (1982) argued that these must be innate because all normal infants show these emotions from a very early age and all cultures interpret the expression of these emotions in the same way. **Secondary emotions** are blends of primary ones and are sometimes culture-specific. For example, the Japanese have an emotion called *hagii* which is a kind of helplessness tinged with anguish. It is apparently not something we experience in the Western world.

Emotional sensitivity

More importantly, there is evidence that infants not only display emotion, which is a highly important factor in their developing relationship with others, but they also *respond* to the emotional expressions of others at an early age. This responsiveness is a crucial element of a relationship. Bonding and attachment are two-way processes.

There is some debate about when infants might be able to do this since newborn infants have a fixed focal length of about 20 cm and therefore might not be able to see emotional expressions clearly (see Figure 2.3). However, what they can see may be sufficient to discern emotions. For example, Bushnell *et al.* (1989) found that most newborn infants showed a preference for their mother's face rather than a stranger's, which suggests sufficient visual discrimination to be able to perform some basic feature analysis which would enable the infant to perceive emotional expressions.

Tronick (1989) certainly found that, by 3 months, infants responded to their mother's facial expressions for happiness, sadness or anger with appropriate expressions. Around the age of 9 months the infant can go one stage further, and use this information to regulate their own social behaviour. This is called **social referencing**.

Shaffer (1993) concluded that 'infant emotions are adaptive in that they promote social contact and help caregivers to adjust their behaviour to the infants' needs and goals. Individuals who cannot interact with the emotions of another will find social relations impossible.

Figure 2.3 A human face as it might appear to a newborn and an older infant

Source: Slater, 1990

Progress exercise

1 How does an infant innately elicit caregiving? Select two possible behaviours and for each suggest in what way this is probably innate.
2 How does the caregiver respond innately? Select two possible behaviours and for each suggest in what way this is probably innate.

This strikes a chord with a possible explanation for **autistic** behaviour. Baron-Cohen *et al.* (1985) suggested that the characteristic social isolation of autistic children may be due to the fact that they lack a **theory of mind**, the ability to comprehend that other people have separate mental states, and therefore lack the ability to engage in emotional relationships.[1]

. . . .
1 For more on autism see *Psychopathology* by Stirling and Hellewell, published in this series.

Learned social abilities

When a group of adults stand over a baby's crib and they all coo, 'Isn't he lovely', some of you may feel 'They don't really think that, they're just saying it because they feel they ought to.' Clearly some of our responses to babies are learned. We do it because it is the norm in our society.

The same is true of babies. They are learning from the moment they are born, and before that. From the very beginning their behaviours are **reinforced**. The baby gurgles and immediately several faces appear over the cot. How nice! The baby likes attention. A while later the baby does it again, and the faces reappear. The baby is being positively reinforced.

Babies are also negatively reinforced. An infant might pee all over his/her mother, who immediately puts the baby down rather angrily. This may have the effect of making this behaviour less likely. I say 'may' because sometimes when adults are angry they give other signals which suggest they aren't really *that* angry and are actually rather amused. In which case the baby is positively reinforced!

Nature and nurture

As infants' behaviour changes as they get older, we cannot be certain whether the cause of the behaviour is nature or nurture – or both. It may be the result of the child learning something new or it may be because the biological system has **matured** and is now capable of new behaviours.

For example, the increasing ability to respond to emotional expressions may be due to learning to fine tune responses as a result of experience, or it may be a function of maturation in the focusing abilities of the visual system. In reality it is very difficult to separate what is due to learning and what is due to maturation (i.e. still genetically determined).

An interest in faces

In a classic experiment, Fantz (1961) demonstrated that **neonates** are able to discriminate between various patterns and most interestingly showed a preference for (or interest in) faces. How could he tell what

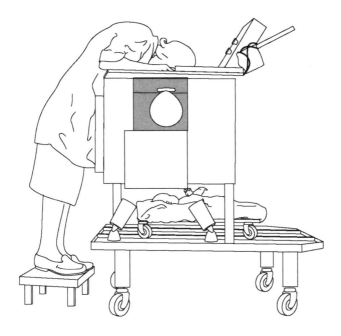

Figure 2.4 Drawing of Fantz's apparatus
Source: After Fantz, 1961

the infants preferred? He built a special 'looking chamber' (see figure 2.4) where infants could lie down on their backs and watch objects hung from the ceiling. An observer recorded the attention time given to each object. This is called the visual preference technique. Fantz found that infants as young as 2 days old spent more time looking at complex patterns than plain coloured shapes, and more time looking at a schematic face than any other patterns.

However, it might have been that the face was just a more complex pattern. To test this hypothesis Fantz jumbled up the facial features (see Figure 2.5) and still found a distinct preference for the correctly organised facial features. (We should note that the term 'preference' may be misleading and 'interest' might be more appropriate since people often look at things not because they like them but because they arouse curiosity, as in looking at a car accident.)

This 'facial preference' finding has been replicated in a number of studies, such as Goren *et al.* (1975) who used slightly different heads in their study (see Figure 2.5). It is possible that these preferences are due to an initial innate interest in human faces, which would make sense. How else could an infant interact with the right class of objects unless it could recognise them in the first place? On the other hand, it is also possible that babies learn, very early on, to like faces because they are positively reinforced. Babies may initially smile at anything but only one class of objects smiles back and this is reinforcing. It is also possible that these findings can be explained in terms of infants simply having a preference for symmetrical patterns.

More and more smiles

Whenever it is that a baby first starts to smile, there is no doubt that once it starts smiling this then increases with age. This is the result of positive reinforcement. Research which has looked at blind babies supports this insofar as they smile *less* than sighted infants as they get older. At birth, blind infants smile as much as their non-blind peers but they receive no visual reinforcement and this probably restricts their smile development (Freeman, 1974).

It is interesting to note that institutionalised infants also show 'smile differences' For example Ambrose (1961) found a delay of about one month in institutionalised infants. Unlike blind babies, institutionalised infants probably receive no positive reinforcement whereas blind babies would at least receive non-visual reinforcement of their smiles.

Reciprocal relationships

One feature of the social interactions described above is the extent to which the caregiver and infant interact. In the past, some psychologists have painted the picture of the infant as a rather passive receptacle for care and information. In fact the child is actively shaping both its environment and social interactions. By the age of 3 weeks an infant behaves differently with an object than it does with a human. This recognition and sense of interaction is vitally important for cognitive and emotional development.

Brazelton *et al.* (1975) suggested that caretaker–infant interactions

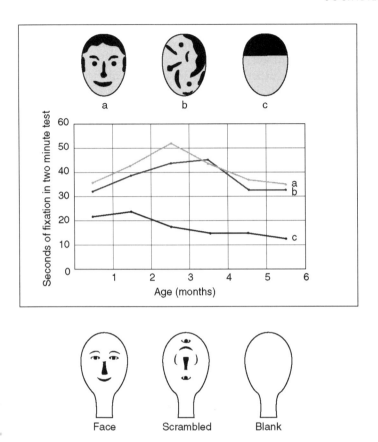

**Figure 2.5 Stimulus pictures for research into infant visual prefer-
ence and graph showing babies' fixation times for the
three face-like stimuli**

**Source: After Fantz, 1961 – top graph and 3 faces; Goven *et al.*,
1975 – bottom 3 faces**

are like a dance because each participant follows and responds to the
other's moves. They observed 12 mother–infant pairs over the first
five months of the infants' lives. Both the mothers' and the infants'
faces were videotaped during play sessions lasting about seven
minutes. The interaction showed cycles: an attention phase with
progressively more responsiveness to the mother's cues, followed by

19

turning away and finally a recovery phase. This rhythm of attention and non-attention occurred several times a minute. They called this **interactional synchrony**.

In a second experiment they deliberately distorted the normal interaction, asking mothers to behave unresponsively, as a means of testing whether the infant was behaving intentionally. The infant's reaction to an unresponsive face was to become visibly concerned, trying at first to get the mother's attention. Eventually, some infants responded by withdrawing into an attitude of helplessness: face averted, body curled up and motionless. This is reminiscent of Seligman's (1975) concept of **learned helplessness**. The infant who finds no response to his behaviour learns *helplessness*. In the same way that an adult does, the infant learns to stop trying to respond.

Brazelton's research demonstrated that very young infants are responsive to adult signals and are active participants in the interaction. Such attentional cycles are critical because they mean the infant can *control* the information they are receiving. Otherwise they might be overwhelmed by the vast amount of incoming information. Stern (1977) observed that over-reaction to an infant may be equally as harmful as under-reaction. In the case of one infant, every time it looked at its mother she reportedly went immediately into high gear, displaying loud and exaggerated facial and vocal social behaviours. The infant averted its gaze but the mother persisted. The infant had no control and ultimately began behaving in an autistic (asocial) manner, for example avoiding eye contact.

Ethical and methodological issues

One feature of the research described in this chapter is that the experimental manipulations often involved causing distress to the infants. For example, in one study by Papousek and Papousek (1975) where mothers left their infants and returned, the infants' increasing rejection of their mothers alarmed the researchers sufficiently to stop their study before completion. This might lead us seriously to question the manipulation used by Brazelton *et al.*, and also to understand why so much of the research in this area has focused on small-scale, non-experimental studies of deprived children where no deliberate manipulation is involved (see Chapter 5).

There are other issues to consider when evaluating this research, of a methodological nature. For instance we should think of the reliability of assessing infant behaviour. Can we be sure that their behaviour was not influenced by the experimenter's expectations? We could also ask whether attention is a reasonable measure of interest.

Progress exercise

1   Suggest how nature and nurture might *interact* in the development of crying.
2   Why is it important that the infant–caregiver relationship is reciprocal?

Individual differences

Sociability is a feature of each individual's **temperament**. At the start of this chapter, I noted that infants differ in terms of their desire to interact with others. This individual difference is in part innate and in part learned.

Innate factors

Sociability has been identified as one of the basic five innate personality characteristics along with activity level, irritability or emotionality, soothability and fearfulness (Goldsmith *et al.*, 1987).

Support for the inherited view comes from studies of identical and non-identical twins, sometimes referred to as monozygotic, MZ, or dizygotic, DZ, twins because MZ twins come from one zygote or egg whereas DZ twins come from two zygotes. MZ twins are genetically identical and therefore, if a trait is inherited, we would expect to find that MZ twins are more similar in terms of this trait than DZ twins, and DZ twins more than genetically unrelated infants. Matheny (1983) found that MZ twins are indeed more similar in their sociability. It could be that parents expect MZ twins to be more similar and their expectations influence the twins' behaviour. However, Scarr

(1968) found that MZ twins were more similar in terms of sociability even when they had been mistakenly reared as DZ twins.

The influence of others

A child's degree of sociability may be a function of how securely attached they are to their caregiver(s) and therefore freer to explore the social and physical world, as we will see later in this book. They will have greater confidence as compared with an insecurely attached child who may be more anxious and fearful when with others. Of course, security of attachment may be related to innate sociability in the first place so it is hard to determine cause and effect.

A further factor in individual differences in sociability may be the extent to which parents encourage their child to be sociable, and also act as good sociable models. Children imitate their loved ones and if, for example, their parents seem anxious when visitors appear, then the child will tend to learn such behaviour.

Parents also teach children how to behave in social situations, and such etiquette is important when the child is being sociable. Children who can't agree to rules with their peers or who push other children around tend to be rejected quite quickly and labelled as unsociable. MacDonald and Parke (1984) suggested that playful interactions between parents and children are important in teaching children how to interact with others. Children whose parents are directive and controlling playmates, tend to be the same in their play with peers.

Finally we might consider how a child's position in a family may influence how sociable they become. Shaffer (1993) reported that first-born children tend to be more sociable and outgoing than later-borns. This is possibly because they are likely to receive more attention when younger and therefore develop greater confidence. On the other hand, Shaffer also noted that some research has found the opposite – that later-borns are more likeable. This could be because they have to learn to cooperate with older, more powerful siblings and this helps with their peer interactions.

Summary

Both infants and adults are innately programmed to be sociable. Infant behaviours, such as their facial features, smiles, cries and emotional sensitivity, all contribute to the formation of early, important relationships and attachments. These innate tendencies go on to be quickly shaped by experience, such as positive and negative reinforcements and imitation of the behaviour of others. Nature and nurture interact.

Sociability and social interaction are reciprocal systems of mutual demands between infants and adults – all participants are equally active and involved. Individual differences must not be overlooked and these too can be explained in terms of both nature and nurture.

Select two of the empirical studies presented in this chapter and, for each:

- describe the study
- state the conclusions
- suggest one criticism in terms of ethical or practical concerns.

Review exercise

Further reading

Schaffer, H.R. (1971) *The growth of sociability*. Harmondsworth: Penguin. Now out of print but an excellent library resource specifically suited to this part of the syllabus, even though the material is not up-to-date.

3

Imprinting and bonding

Introduction

We speak of forming a bond with another person, a bond of friend-ship or a bond of love. A bond is something which ties things or people together. Bonding is a first step in forming a relationship.

It is often used to mean an attachment, for example psychologists speak of 'attachment bonds'. However, as I suggested in the introductory chapter of this book, we can make a subtle distinction between the *bonding* process, which is part of the initial stages of relationship formation, and the *attachments* which are the ultimate end of this process. To my mind, bonding is less of a **cognitive** or mental process than attachment, which is why psychologists largely talk about bonding in some non-human animals and attachment in primates and humans, and bonding in the early weeks and months of infant development.

Imprinting

Imprinting is a concept brought to psychology by ethologists whose central argument, as I have explained before, is that any characteristic which increases an individual's chances of successful reproduction (and survival is a crucial aspect of this) will be more likely to remain in the species' **gene pool**. Individuals who possess characteristics which do not enhance survival are less likely to be around. Therefore, if we observe the behaviours and characteristics of the animals who are around us we can surmise that these characteristics are likely in some way to be adaptive, or at 'worst' neutral (because neutral features are neither selected for or against). Imprinting is one such behaviour.

Konrad Lorenz and greylag geese

Konrad Lorenz is one of the most widely known ethologists. There were others before him but Lorenz played a key role in popularising ethology, most notably through his book *King Solomon's Ring* (1952). In it he recorded his observations of geese, mallard ducks, cats, hedgehogs, horses, fish ... accompanied by enchanting line drawings of his subjects (see Figure 3.1). The most famous of his observations, with greylag geese, was originally reported in an article published in German in 1935. Lorenz demonstrated a fact commonly known to farmers that when such animals are born without a mother, the young will form a bond with whatever animal is present and adopt this animal as their 'mother'. This bond can be demonstrated through the **following response** (also called **filial imprinting**), a response which can only occur in **precocial** species, those whose young are mobile shortly after birth.

Lorenz (1935) divided a clutch of greylag goose eggs into two groups. One group was left with their natural mother, the other eggs were kept in an incubator. When the latter group hatched, the first living (moving) thing they saw was Lorenz and they soon started following him around. Lorenz marked the two groups to distinguish them and placed them together with their mother. The goslings quickly divided themselves up, one following their natural mother and Lorenz's brood following him.

Figure 3.1 Some of the drawings from Lorenz's *King Solomon's Ring* which presents an ethologist's view of animal behaviour
Source: Lorenz, 1952

Critical period hypothesis

The concept of a **critical period** comes from embryology. An embryo is the earliest stage of prenatal development. At this time of development certain events must take place during a particular window of time or they won't happen at all. For example, in human development the arms begin to develop between day 24 and 26. Any interference with development at this critical stage will permanently affect the limb's development – it won't happen.

Lorenz felt that this concept of a critical period described the restricted period of time during which he believed that imprinting took place. Hess (1958) found that ducks showed the strongest following response (imprinting) between 13 and 16 hours after hatching and that, thereafter, the imprint was irreversible. Furthermore, 32 hours after hatching, the ducklings showed almost no ability to acquire a following response if they hadn't acquired one already. This suggested that imprinting occurs during a critical period and once this has passed, it can no longer take place.

Sensitive period

Other psychologists later suggested that the idea of a critical period was perhaps rather too strong and it would be more appropriate to describe this as a **sensitive period**. It was the psychologist Sluckin (1965) who first coined this phrase in the light of his own and other research which showed that even though imprinting was less likely outside this period, it still could occur.

Supra-individual

Another feature of imprinting is that it is **supra-individual**, which means that the actual process of imprinting, and the drive to do it, is innate but there is flexibility about the class of objects which is imprinted on. In other words it is beyond the level of the individual thing (thus 'supra-individual'). Lorenz found that his goslings would imprint on a cardboard box, a flashing light or a rubber ball. Guiton (1966) imprinted leghorn chicks on a yellow rubber glove. There is no commonality among these objects aside from the fact they are visual stimuli, and that they were present during a sensitive period.

Lorenz found that not all birds species imprinted on visual stimuli, as the goslings had. For example:

> I remembered I had once let a muscovy duck hatch a clutch of mallard eggs [and they] failed to accept this foster mother. As soon as they were dry, they had simply run away from her and I had trouble enough catching these crying, erring children. On the other hand, I once let a fat white farmyard duck hatch out mallards and the little wild things ran just as happily after her as if she had been their real mother. The secret must have lain in her call note.
>
> (Lorenz, 1952)

There is some echo here of the research described in the previous chapter on the human neonate's preference for human faces. Animals would also appear to have some innate species-specific preferences.

Consequences of imprinting

In precocial species the following response (which maintains proximity between caregiver and young) is a main consequence of imprinting. It obviously helps ensure the safety of the young. It is also desirable (and adaptive) for young to spend time with other members of their species in order to learn how to eventually look after themselves. The young learn from and imitate the behaviour of adults in many other ways, for example if sparrows are reared in isolation they fail to develop their adult birdsong (Marler and Mundinger, 1971).

Imprinting is also crucial in later identification of a suitable mate. If an individual mates with a member of another species, they may produce offspring but the offspring are invariably sterile, as is the case with mules (the product of a horse and a donkey). Therefore it is important to be able to identify a member of your own species – if you don't, you don't reproduce successfully. Immelman (1972) demonstrated the role of imprinting in an experiment where zebra finches were reared by Bengalese finches, and vice versa. The finches preferred to mate with their foster species even when given a free choice. This is called **sexual imprinting**.

In humans a similar thing has been observed and called the **Westermarck effect** after Westermarck (1891) who noted that, if children spend considerable time together before the age of 6 (a sensitive period), they avoid subsequently forming sexual relationships with these individuals, a kind of reverse imprinting. This would clearly be useful in avoiding incest. Incest is non-adaptive because the offspring of such unions have a greater chance of developing recessive genetic disorders. There is evidence to support the Westermarck effect. For instance, Shepher (1971) found that not one of the 3,000 Israeli marriage records he studied was between individuals who had been raised together on the same **kibbutz**.

Evaluation

I have covered only some of the key features of imprinting here, for more information you could look at the books recommended in the 'further reading'. To summarise: the claims are that imprinting occurs during a sensitive period, it is supra-individual, very rapid, irreversible and has lasting consequences.

There is some dispute, however, over these characteristics. The original concept of imprinting, that an encounter with an appropriate object led to the image of that object being somehow stamped irreversibly on the nervous system, was for many years the accepted view of imprinting. Now it is understood that imprinting is a more 'plastic and forgiving mechanism' (Hoffman, 1996). For example, Guiton

(1966) found that he could reverse the imprinting in chickens who initially tried to mate with the rubber gloves. He found that later, after spending time with their own species, they were able to engage in normal sexual behaviour with their own kind.

It is also thought that imprinting may not after all be so very different from any other kind of learning. Learning can also can take place rapidly, with little conscious effort. It is also fairly irreversible.

Perhaps the key feature of imprinting is that it is a form of learning which takes place *best* at a particular time in development. It is an innate readiness to learn during a special or sensitive period. It may be explained in terms of the production of **endorphins**, the body's own form of morphine. Hoffman (1996) suggested that certain objects, or features of the object, provide stimulation which is pleasurable and this stimulates the production of endorphins which create a state of arousal which is optimal for learning.

The importance of imprinting research, in the context of this book, is that many of these issues apply to attachment, such as sensitive periods and irreversibility. We will return to them again later.

One final, important point of evaluation is the consideration of **ethics**. Shortly we will look at research which involved monkeys, where they experienced permanent damage as a result of emotional deprivation. Such manipulation of their early experience is clearly questionable but the same can be said of the imprinting research. How far was it acceptable to manipulate the impressionable young of any species for the purpose of serious scientific interest? We may laugh at the idea of chicks imprinted on yellow gloves but there is a serious concern about such experimentation.

Progress exercise

1   Identify two pieces of evidence that support the validity of the concept of imprinting.
2   Identify two pieces of evidence which suggest that the concept lacks validity.
3   Name two benefits of imprinting to the offspring.
4   Name one benefit of imprinting to the parent.

Bonding in non-human animals

Harry Harlow conducted and supervised a series of psychological experiments related to the emotional development of rhesus monkeys. Harlow's original interest was in learning and he used the monkeys in his learning experiments. In order to reduce the mortality rate of his experimental subjects he separated infant monkeys from their mothers, enabling him to maintain a better standard of physical care. He and his co-workers noticed that the young monkeys became particularly distressed when their cages were cleaned. The cages had 'sanitary pads' lining the bottom and it appeared that the monkeys became attached to these as a kind of 'security blanket'.

In the 1950s the dominant doctrine in psychology was **behaviourism**, which held that attachment was related to feeding. Behaviourists proposed that the infant forms a bond with its caregiver because that individual satisfies their hunger and thus gives them pleasure. The infant associates this pleasure with their caregiver and this was assumed to lead to a positive bond (positive reinforcement). However, Harlow's experience with his experimental monkeys led him to believe that the process of bonding may in fact be more related to other physical comforts rather than just feeding (which is in a sense a physical comfort).

Wire mothers

To test this hypothesis Harlow devised an experiment where single infant monkeys were caged with two dummy 'mothers' for the first eight months of their lives (Harlow, 1958; Harlow and Zimmerman, 1959). One dummy was made out of a wire-mesh cylinder with a monkey-like face and feeding bottle attached, the other identical wire-mesh dummy had no feeding bottle and was wrapped in soft towelling (see Figure 3.2).

Harlow found that the monkeys spent most time with their cloth mother and only went to the other mother for food. When they were frightened they went to their cloth mother. This seems clear support against the behaviourist view that it is the 'hand that feeds' which matters, though in another way the data is still consistent with behaviourism insofar as there is still a reinforcer but one which is protection/comfort rather than food. On the other hand, body

Figure 3.2   Photographs showing how Harlow's monkeys used the cloth mother for comfort and fed from the wire 'mother'

Source: Harlow, 1959

contact could be understood in terms of adaptive value – a body can protect against danger whereas food can't.

Clearly the monkeys received only a poor version of body contact, one which lacked *interaction* and, not surprisingly, they grew up to be socially maladjusted and displayed autistic-like behaviour. For example, they were very detached from their environment, displayed repetitive stereotyped movements (a characteristic of **autism**), and behaved in a hostile manner towards others and towards their own bodies.

Experimental variations

Harlow and his colleagues went on to test their hypothesis in a variety of other ways. Harlow and Harlow (1962) reported that the monkeys subsequently had difficulty mating and became abusive and rejecting mothers. However, if the isolation was stopped before the monkeys were three months old, the ill effects disappeared.

They tried raising some 'orphan' young monkeys together to see if the effects were due to isolation or specifically to maternal deprivation. The monkeys spent most of the early months huddled together but appeared to develop normally. Novak and Harlow (1975) raised infant monkeys in total isolation for a year and then placed them with younger, normally reared monkeys who played and interacted with the abnormally reared ones. The isolated monkeys responded quite well to this therapy and appeared to recover from their earlier deprivation.

Rosenblum and Harlow (1963) offered monkeys two types of cloth mother, one who blasted the infants with compressed air at random intervals. They found that the infants showed the strongest attachments to this punitive 'mother', a finding which might be relevant to the relationship between abused children and their parents because it is otherwise hard to understand why such children remain attached to their abusive parents.

Other researchers have found similar results. For instance, Hogg *et al.* (1994) examined the effects of a 24-week separation on three infant gorillas who had been living with their mothers. During separation, the infants' behaviour initially showed threat responses and increased locomotion, characteristic behaviours of the protest stage of **anaclitic depression**. Upon reunion, the infants did not immediately engage in attachment behaviours with their mothers and spent more time in contact with each other.

Conclusions

There are three points to note. First, the evidence suggests that bonding results from body contact rather feeding. Second, this contact needs to be interactive rather than passive, otherwise emotional development is abnormal. Third, the lack of an interactive attachment figure can be compensated for by the presence of others such as peers, or rather, peers can be alternative attachment figures.

Evaluation of non-human research

There is an obvious tendency to compare non-human primate behaviour with human behaviour and make generalisations, but we must be wary. Behaviourists would argue that the differences between non-human animals and humans are only ones of 'degree' and there-fore the same principles apply to both groups of animals. Other psychologists, such as Bowlby (1969), feel that there are qualitative differences in terms of things such as consciousness, language and the great diversity of cultures in human but not non-human species. This suggests that we should be cautious about generalising from non-human research to human behaviour. On the other hand, Suomi (1976) argued that one could use monkey behaviour as a *model* for certain basic human psychopathologies such as depression, and that we should treat the non-human evidence with prudence but it is not irrelevant.

Ethical considerations are important as well, as we noted earlier. One could claim that the early research by Harlow was justifiable because he simply had no idea of the consequences of his initial experiments. However the same defence cannot be made for subse-quent research which clearly caused the animals and their caregivers significant and sometimes permanent distress.

Progress exercise

1   Imagine you work in a zoo, looking after primates. One of the young animals appears very withdrawn. What remedy might you suggest and why?
2   Select one criticism of primate research and present an argument for and against this view.

Bonding in humans

I have suggested that the bonding process in humans is the beginning of the attachment relationship. Some psychologists and paediatri-cians have studied the very earliest experiences, around the time of birth, which may be critical in bond formation.

Skin-to-skin contact

The sensitive period hypothesis suggests that there are periods in development when an individual is maximally sensitive to learn certain things, such as imprinting on a mother-figure (and the mother's imprinting on her offspring). Klaus and Kennell (1976) focused on the bond formed between mothers and their newborn infants in the period immediately after birth. It had become the hospital practice in this country to organise childbirth so that an infant was quickly removed from its mother immediately after birth, for such things as weighing and other checks. The infant was then returned to its mother for only a brief period, cleaned and swaddled in blankets. Many mothers would have had little close physical contact with their infants in the first hours or even days, especially if they were not breastfeeding.

Klaus and Kennell believed that there is a sensitive period in the bonding process just at this time and that this relied on skin-to-skin contact. If this was correct, removing infants from their mothers could well have interfered in this natural process.

To test their hypothesis, they arranged for one group of fourteen randomly selected mothers to follow the 'traditional' approach to neonatal care – they saw their babies briefly after delivery, visited them six to twelve hours later in the hospital nursery and fed them on a four-hourly routine. A second group of mothers had 'extended contact' with their infants. They spent an extra five hours a day cuddling their infants, including skin-to-skin contact. One month later, Klaus and Kennell found that the mothers in the extended contact group were physically closer to their infants and more soothing than those in the traditional group. A year later, the same group still did more cuddling and, moreover, the infants scored higher on tests of physical and mental development.

Klaus and Kennell (1982) suggested that **hormones** which are present at the time of birth focus the mother's attention on her baby and make *her* more susceptible to forming an attachment. Indeed, Trevarthan (1979) found unusually high levels of endorphins present in both mothers and their infants during and immediately after delivery. If a bond is not formed during this hormonal surge, then the mother and infant may form a less strong bond, an outcome which will ultimately affect the attachment process.

Klaus and Kennell (1982) also suggested that fathers will benefit in terms of attachment from being present during this sensitive period.

Evaluation

There are two strands to this argument. First, that caregivers do not become as attached to their infants if they miss out on this early contact. Second, that infants need close physical contact during a sensitive period to maximise their bond formation, which forms the basis for later attachment. Note the reciprocal nature of this argument.

A number of other studies retested the hypothesis. Goldberg (1983), in a review of these, concluded that the effects of early bonding were not as large nor as long-lasting as Klaus and Kennell's original research suggested. For instance, Myers (1984) observed infants with their mothers and found that, after nine days the early-contact mothers were neither more affectionate nor more responsive than the mothers who had no extended contact. On the other hand, De Chateau and Wiberg (1977) found support for the value of extended contact. In their study it was found that mothers who had skin-to-skin contact with their unwashed babies immediately after birth, and also put the baby to their breast to 'suckle' engaged in significantly more kissing and embracing with their infants, and breastfed on average for two and a half months longer than 'traditional contact' mothers.

We should remember that adoptive parents and their children, and premature infants kept in incubators and their parents, form very strong emotional ties despite a lack of this early contact.

The conclusion is that early contact may well be desirable and may create strong attachments more readily and reliably, but it is not a sufficient or necessary precursor for strong attachments.

Ethical and practical concerns

Much of this chapter has focused on non-human animal research, and perhaps for a good reason. It is very difficult to conduct well-controlled experiments with humans especially human neonates. The research methods used in human studies are often criticised for their lack of adequate experimental control, such as adequate control groups. In order to have **control groups**, one would have to deny certain parents and their children treatments which might be beneficial (such as skin-to-skin contact). There are also practical research problems, such as deciding on how to measure the outcome of any experimental treatment. The **Strange Situation** is one method of doing this (see p. 44).

What bonding research means for attachment

As you have been reading this chapter describing various empirical studies of imprinting and bonding, you may have begun to formulate a theory of bonding and attachment (remember that a theory may be no more than an organised set of ideas which make sense of a collection of facts). Animals, human and non-human, appear to be born with innate abilities to (1) attract attachment and (2) to become attached. Both infants and caregivers have many behaviours which facilitate this process. The bond provides a number of useful functions and is adaptive. This is the positive side of attachment.

The negative side of attachment is apparent when individuals are prevented from forming such bonds. There may be some quite extreme consequences of bond prevention and disruption, which further supports the idea that such bonds are crucial for healthy development.

Summary

The concept of imprinting has been used to understand the process of bonding. It is an innate predisposition in precocial animals to learn during a sensitive period, which may be related to endorphins. It is a predisposition which leads young animals to follow a caregiver and learn sexual preferences. Imprinting is supra-individual, rapid and lasting, however it is probably not irreversible nor distinctly different from learning more generally.

Studies of primates, by Harlow for example, have shown that the bonding process is related to body contact. If the bonding process is disrupted, the young primate may become depressed and suffer long-term emotional effects. Generalisation from non-human to human behaviour must be done cautiously.

There may also be a sensitive period in human infant–caregiver bonding when skin-to-skin extended contact is important, which again may be related to the production of hormones.

Human and non-human research is faced with methodological and ethical problems.

1 Here is a list of concepts. Tick which group(s) the concept applies to.

Concept	Lower animals	Non-human primates	Humans
Critical period			
Sensitive period			
Anaclitic depression			
Visual contact			
Vocal contact			
Feeding			
Need for bodily contact			
Imprinting			
Bonding			
Attachment			

2 List the behaviours which are thought to facilitate the process of imprinting and/or bonding.

Further reading

Hoffman, H.S. (1996) *Amorous turkeys and addicted ducklings: a search for the causes of social attachment.* Author's Cooperative. An unusual book providing interesting details about imprinting plus descriptions of some of the people in imprinting research as well as information about the research process.

Klaus, M.H., Kennell, J.H. and Klaus, P.H. (1995) *Bonding: building the foundations of secure attachment and independence.* London: Cedar. Thorough and up-to-date paperback written for parents and caregivers about many different aspects of the bonding process.

4

The attachment process

Introduction

In the last chapter, we looked at bonding, which I suggested is the beginning of the attachment process. In this chapter we will look at the continuing formation of attachments through infancy, considering the benefits and consequences of healthy attachments and how the quality of these attachments can be measured. This account will be mainly from the infant's point of view, though we should remember at all times that attachment is a two-way involvement.

What is attachment?

Schaffer and Emerson (1964) defined it as 'the tendency of the young to seek the proximity of certain other members of the species'.

Maccoby (1980) identified four characteristic behaviours: seeking proximity to primary caregiver, distress on separation, pleasure when reunited, and general orientation of behaviour towards primary caregiver.

We can see from these definitions that proximity is a key feature, and that this can be maintained with respect to any other person or thing. A field study by Anderson (1972) illustrates this aspect of attachment. He observed children in a London park and noticed that it was rare indeed to see a child under the age of 3 who wandered further than 200 feet from his mother before returning, perhaps just to touch her knee or come close. Attachment is like a piece of invisible string.

A second, key aspect of attachment is its interactive nature. Maurer and Maurer (1989) wrote 'Attachments are not formed by a congenital glue held in limited supply: They are welded in the heat of interactions.' In other words, attachments depend on interaction rather than two people just being together.

The development of attachment behaviour

Schaffer and Emerson (1964) conducted an extensive study of Scottish infants from birth to the age of 18 months. This research is described in detail in the key research summaries section of Chapter 10 (see p. 135). The data they collected have been used repeatedly and, even though this study has been superseded in some details, their general framework holds up. They suggested a stage theory of attachment development under the following headings, here presented with the addition of more recent information.

1 The asocial stage

In the first month of life Schaffer and Emerson suggested that infants produce similar responses to all objects, whether they are animate or inanimate. As we have seen in the last chapter, infants of this age prefer human faces but these need not be 'live' (i.e. responding) ones. They also react to human voices and show some recognition of their main caregiver(s) in terms of being more settled when held by such persons or giving a broader smile when they hear a familiar voice.

During this time the infant is bonding with its caregivers but has not, as yet, formed attachments.

It may be erroneous to think of this as an asocial stage, which suggests that the infant is oblivious to the social dimension. In fact, as we have seen in Chapter 2, the infant is extremely sociable. However, its ability to respond socially is restricted by general immobility and a lack of coordination. Neonates may well recognise their own mother (Bushnell *et al.*, 1989) but they are equally comforted by any other person. In this sense they are asocial.

Towards the end of this period, infants are beginning to show a greater preference for social stimuli, such as a smiling face, and to be more content when they are with people.

2 Indiscriminate attachments

From 2 to 7 months infants become more social. They prefer human company and can distinguish between familiar and unfamiliar people. However, they are still relatively easily comforted by anyone, and do not yet show anxiety with strangers. The most distinctive feature of this stage is their general sociability.

3 Specific attachments

Around 7 months of age infants begin to show a distinctly different sort of protest when one particular person puts them down. Equally, they show especial joy at reunion with that person and are most comforted by this main caregiver. They are said to have formed a specific attachment. Around the same time, the infant begins to display **stranger anxiety**, an uneasiness with strangers. It is no longer possible to leave the infant with just anyone without them showing distress.

4 Multiple attachments

Very soon after the main attachment is formed, the infant also develops a wider circle of attachments depending on how many consistent relationships he/she has. Such attachments might be with mothers or fathers (depending on who the main attachment was with), siblings, grandparents, a childminder or other close family

EARLY SOCIALISATION

friends. The quality of these attachments is a matter of some debate. Some psychologists believe that there remains one special attachment figure. Other psychologists have suggested that all attachments are equivalent though qualitatively different. We will return to this issue later in the chapter.

Understanding why these changes take place

These developments can be understood in terms of the infant's cognitive development. Perceptually, their visual system is progressively becoming more and more capable of making the fine distinctions which are necessary to recognise familiar faces. Ahrens (1954) found that very young children will smile at a drawing with no features except two eyes. By 4 months they smile most at a picture with just eyes and a nose. By 7 months they show greater interest in a face which is not just a schematic drawing of a face but shaded to look more like the real thing.

The infant's **schemas** have also developed. Schemas are packets of information which act as representations of the world. With experience, the infant has developed schemas for some of the things around him or her, and gradually these schemas have become more elaborate so the infant can now distinguish not just between what is human and not human, but between various people that he or she knows and doesn't know.

A final feature of cognitive development which is worth considering is the infant's sense of **object permanence** (Piaget 1970). Young infants fail to appreciate that, once something is out of sight, it hasn't ceased to exist. There is some debate at what age the infant does learn object permanence[1] but there is a point when they do come to realise that what is out of sight is actually still there, somewhere. You can demonstrate this yourself if you try to play the game of peepo with a very young child – they are not interested. Once the infant has acquired a sense of object permanence we can see that, when the caregiver leaves the room, the infant now continues to watch for the caregiver's return rather than instantly turning his or her attention to something else.

We should also consider physical development. It is no accident that the time when specific attachments develop in human infants is also the

1 See the book in this series on 'cognitive development' by David Cohen.

42

time when they become mobile. If they didn't become anxious about being on their own, they might easily become separated from caregivers. It is interesting to note that Ainsworth (1967) found that Ugandan babies expressed stranger anxiety at the slightly earlier age of 6 months and that their motor development was more advanced.

Evaluation

Stage theories are always somewhat dangerous because they suggest a kind of 'fixedness' about human development, whereas it is actually relatively fluid. Some psychologists have preferred to use other terms such as 'phases' instead of 'stages' to reflect this. In the case of 'stages' in the development of attachment the key point is the sequence of events rather than the actual ages at which the stages might or might not occur.

Having said this, notional ages are useful in identifying possibly abnormal development such as autism. A child who has not formed attachments by the age of a year would certainly give cause for concern. Investigations would look at the caregivers as well as the child since attachment is a mutual process.

Individual differences in attachment

In the chapter on sociability we saw how the infant's temperament, or innate personality, is an important factor in the extent to which the infant interacts with their social world. Thomas and Chess (1977), in their classic study of innate temperament, identified three basic infant personality types: easy, difficult and slow-to-warm-up. It is quite possible that children form more secure relationships simply because they have an 'easy' temperament whereas difficult children are likely to form insecure relationships.

Caregivers also come to the attachment situation with a particular personality (a product of nature and nurture) which will either facilitate or not facilitate the attachment process. In addition to this, there are further factors, such as the immediate circumstances surrounding the infant's birth as we saw in Klaus and Kennell's research on bonding.

Finally, the **fit** between caregiver and child is important. When two personalities happen to clash, attachment may be poor, as would be the case when a child who likes to be cuddled ends up with a parent who doesn't like cuddling.

Progress exercise

Tommy, age 1 year old, is now more securely attached to his father than he was six months previously.

1   Suggest one reason why Tommy's age might be an important factor in the development of his attachment.
2   Describe one way in which Tommy's experience might have been an important factor in his attachment to his father.

Measuring attachment

All of the research examined so far depends on having some means of measuring attachment. Schaffer and Emerson (1964) developed a method to measure strength of attachment (see page 136). Ainsworth and her colleagues (1978) established an experimental and more rigorous way of doing this. Both methods looked at behaviours which are associated with attachment.

Ainsworth's procedure was called the **Strange Situation** and consisted of seven episodes each lasting about three minutes:

1   The mother (or caregiver) carries the infant into a laboratory room. She puts the infant on the floor and sits quietly in a chair. She does not interact with the infant unless the infant seeks her attention.
2   A stranger enters the room and talks with the mother. The stranger gradually approaches the infant with a toy.
3   The mother leaves. If the infant is involved in active play, the stranger observes unobtrusively. If the infant is passive, the stranger tries to interest him or her in a toy. If the infant shows distress (crying) the stranger tries to comfort him or her.
4   The mother returns and the stranger leaves.
5   After the infant has again begun to play, the mother also departs. The infant is left alone briefly.
6   The stranger re-enters the room and behaves as described in 3.
7   The mother returns and the stranger leaves.

Progress exercise

1 At which stages do you think the infant will display anxiety?
2 How do you think a 4-month-old infant would behave when his or her mother leaves the room?
3 How do you think a 7-month-old infant would behave when his or her mother returns to the room?

What the Strange Situation measures

The Strange Situation provides a measure of the security of a child's attachment on the basis of four behaviours:

1 **Separation anxiety**. This is the unease the child shows when left by its caregiver.
2 The infants' willingness to explore. A more securely attached child will explore more widely.
3 Stranger anxiety. Security of attachment is related to *greater* stranger anxiety.
4 Reunion behavior. Insecurely attached children often greet their caregiver's return by ignoring them or behaving ambivalently.

Types of attachment

Ainsworth and other psychologists have used the Strange Situation to determine patterns of attachment:

1 *Secure attachment* (type B). The infant shows a moderate level of seeking closeness to the mother. The infant is upset by her departure but greets her positively on reunion and is readily soothed. This is the optimal type of attachment.
2 *Insecure/avoidant attachment* (type A). The infant shows apparent indifference when the mother leaves, and does not display stranger anxiety. At reunion the infant actively avoids contact with the mother. The mother tends to be insensitive and ignores the infant during play.

3 *Insecure/resistant attachment* (type C). The infant is very distressed when the mother goes and not easily consoled on her return. The infant seeks comfort and rejects it at the same time. The mother's behaviour is also inconsistent, sometimes rejecting and angry towards her baby and sometimes overly responsive and sensitive towards the baby. Exploration tends to be limited as the infant has difficulty separating from the mother.

4 *Insecure/disorganised attachment* (type D). This category was not in Ainsworth's original scheme but has been recognised as an important fourth type of response (Main and Solomon, 1986). The infant shows no set pattern of behaviour at separation or reunion (thus 'disorganised'). This kind of behaviour is associated with abused children or those whose mothers are chronically depressed.

The most important distinction is between secure and insecure attachment. Studies in the United States have tended to find that about 65 per cent of infants are securely attached, with the next largest group being Type C (insecure/resistant). For example Campos *et al.* (1983) suggested the following estimates for American children: secure: 62 per cent, avoidant: 23 per cent, ambivalent: 15 per cent.

Stability of attachment

When considering potential long-term effects of attachments, we must question the stability of attachments. To what extent is an insecure infant still insecure at a later age? In other words, how much do early attachments predict about later emotional behaviour?

Waters (1978) found 90 per cent consistency of classification when infants were tested and retested between the ages of 12 and 18 months. There was some evidence that stability is lower in 'working-class' families, but this could be explained as being due to the fact that their lives were generally less stable across the period of repeated testing.

Main *et al.* (1985) conducted a longitudinal study. Infants were assessed in the Strange Situation before the age of 18 months with both their mothers and fathers. When the children were retested at the age of 6, the researchers found considerable consistency in security of attachment to both parents. 100 per cent of the secure babies were classified as secure at 6 years, and 75 per cent avoidant babies remained in the same classification.

Evaluation

Behaviour in the Strange Situation has been taken to represent differences in *relationships* between infants and their main caregivers. For example, Main and Weston (1981) found that children behaved differently depending on which parent they were with, which indicates that it is the relationship which determines the response in the Strange Situation rather than the infant's temperament.

However, Lamb *et al.* (1984) have questioned this, suggesting that the behaviours shown in the Strange Situation are due more to differences in the infant's temperament and less to the differences in the relationship. Children may display innate differences in basic personality and, in this way, they inspire different patterns of interaction.

In addition there are cultural differences. For example, studies have found more secure attachments in Great Britain (75 per cent) and lower rates in Germany (57 per cent) (Schaffer, 1996). This must mean that parenting behaviours are different, presumably as a result of cultural socialisation.

So we can explain behaviour in the Strange Situation as a combined function of a caregiver and infant's learned behaviour and temperament, and the relationship between both caregiver and child. This once more underlines the interactive nature of the attachment relationship. It is always as well to remember that both partners are part of the socialisation process, an insecurely attached child isn't simply the consequence of an unresponsive parent.

A further consideration is the ethical one. What do we feel about the ethics of this procedure? Is it acceptable to place infants, and caregivers, in mildly or extremely anxious situations? As with all ethical judgements we must weigh the cost against the benefit. Such research has been vitally important in providing a means of measuring infant attachment and understanding situations which cause anxiety, such as hospitalisation or day care.

The value of a secure attachment

We must ask what are the benefits of having a secure rather than an insecure attachment?

Short-term effects: benefits of secure attachment

In the short term the attachment process is important for maintaining proximity between the infant and its caregiver, for safety, food and general care. In a secure relationship both partners find this pleasurable and their mutual pleasure is continually reinforced. You can imagine that, in an insecure relationship caregivers might prefer to avoid their infant's company and their infants might well search for care elsewhere, a cycle of negative reinforcement.

A secure attachment provides a secure base for exploring the world and appears to facilitate early cognitive development. For example, Hazen and Durrett (1982) found that securely attached young children were more independent explorers of their environment and were also more innovative in their approach to problem solving.

Long-term effects: emotional development and relationships

The central theme of this book is that attachment is the basis of emotional development. Bowlby's concept of the **internal working model** was that the attachment relationship created an internal model for all future relationships. The internal working model is a set of conscious and/or unconscious rules regarding our relationships with others.

This would suggest that we would find an association between early and later patterns of attachment. Grossmann and Grossmann (1991) found that children who were securely attached to their mothers as infants enjoyed close friendships later in childhood, whereas those who were avoidant or anxious reported either having no friends or friends whose names they could not remember.

Hazan and Shaver (1987) focused on the relationship between patterns of infant attachment and different styles of adult romantic love. They printed a 'Love Quiz' in a local newspaper and analysed 620 responses from people aged between 14 and 82 years. The researchers classified people as secure, ambivalent or avoidant 'types' based on their description of their childhood experiences, and found patterns of adult styles of romantic love which were consistent with their attachment 'type'. Secure types said they believed in enduring love, they thought others were trustworthy and didn't worry about being abandoned or about their partners being too intimate. Anxious ambivalent types experienced love as a painful preoccupation that never seemed to work out, they worried that their partners didn't really love them or might abandon them. They had many self-doubts and insecurities. Insecure avoidant lovers were even more doubtful about the possibility of love. They feared and avoided closeness with others, and believed that they did not need love to be happy.

Long-term effects: parenting

Quinton and Rutter (1988) studied women who had spent much of their early lives in institutions. They observed how these women interacted with their own children and concluded that they were less sensitive, less supportive and less warm than a group of non-institutionalised women. This result reminds us of Harlow's work with monkeys (see chapter 3). Early attachments enable an individual to form both good parent–child relationships themselves, and provide suitable role models.

Long-term effects: personality development

Other studies have looked at the relationship between early patterns of attachment and subsequent personality characteristics. For example, Erickson *et al.* (1985) conducted the Minnesota Mother–Child Interaction project which looked specifically at children of over 250 'high risk' mothers. The researchers predicted beforehand that these women were more likely to have insecurely attached children because of their demographic characteristics: low *SES*, poor education, mainly single, and living in chaotic conditions. The project found that, in general, anxious babies were less competent in preschool, had more problems with peers, and were more disliked by teachers. Avoidant babies differed the most from secure babies in preschool. They were highly dependent, non-compliant, and poorly skilled in social interactions with peers. They were described by teachers as hostile, impulsive, giving up easily, and withdrawn.

However, the researchers cautioned against making over-generalisations, because they did not find that every anxious baby had problems later and some secure babies did have problems.

Long-term effects: self-esteem

An important aspect of personality is one's self-esteem. Rogers (1961) suggested that 'unconditional positive regard' from one's caregiver frees the individual from striving for social approval and enables them eventually to obtain self-actualisation. Sroufe (1985) found that infants who were securely attached to their mothers became more self-reliant toddlers and had a better sense of self-esteem. Sroufe's study followed infants from birth to the age of 19 years. He found that even if the children had unstable lives, as long as they had a secure mother–infant attachment, they were likely to be self-reliant into adolescence, have lower rates of psychopathology, enjoy successful peer relationships in adolescence and do well in school.

Long-term effects: cognitive development

Attachment is also important in cognitive development because, as we have seen, it provides a secure base for exploration in infancy. Bus and Van IJzendoorn (1988) tested children when they were 2 years old using the Strange Situation, and then three years later assessed the children's reading interests and skills. Preschool teachers also completed a questionnaire about preparatory reading and intelligence. They found that the securely attached children showed more interest in written material than did the insecurely attached children, regardless of their intelligence and the amount of preparatory reading instruction.

Sroufe suggested that infant attachment doesn't directly affect aptitude, but rather it influences confidence, attitude and, subsequently, attendance and achievement.

Another problem with the notion that secure attachment fosters cognitive development is the fact that we are looking at correlations. It is possible that intelligent infants are more likely to become securely attached.

Evaluation

In all of these studies, we should remember that it is unlikely that children's attachments remained the same. Changing home circumstances frequently occur and this would lead to both positive and negative changes in attachments. This makes the correlations potentially meaningless. Furthermore, the studies generally considered only one attachment relationship, some infants may have had secure attachments elsewhere. It may also be that correlations occur because of some other aspect of the parent-child interactional system that is correlated with both Strange Situation behaviour and the personality differences later.

Monotropy versus multiple attachments

Attachments can be considered in terms of the degree of their security or insecurity. A further important question has been whether it is one main caregiver who provides this secure relationship, or whether the infant has multiple relationships which are all on a par and of equal importance.

Monotropy

Bowlby (1951) introduced the term **monotropy**, meaning turning towards one person. He proposed that attachment occurs with a single person, usually but not necessarily the mother, and that this unique bond had special significance, 'it is because of this marked tendency to monotropy that we are capable of deep feelings' (Bowlby, 1988).

The case for multiple attachments

Bowlby did not suggest that monotropy was absolute but that the child has a hierarchy of attachments. His later views were influenced in part by Schaffer and Emerson (1964) who found that almost a third of the infants in their study showed attachment behaviour towards more than one person almost from the moment when they first formed specific attachments. By the age of 18 months 87 per cent had formed multiple attachments to fathers, siblings, grandparents and so on.

Another study by Ainsworth (1967) looked at attachment in the Ganda tribe of Uganda. Here she also found evidence of multiple attachments (see Chapter 7 on cultural differences).

There is no doubt that infants form several attachments and that these are all beneficial probably exactly because of their qualitative differences. For example, fathers' style of play is more often physically stimulating and unpredictable whereas mothers are more likely to hold their infants, soothe them, attend to their needs and read them stories (Parke, 1981). On the other hand, Field (1978) found that when fathers were the primary caregiver they also acted in a more nurturing and gentle fashion. This suggests that the differences may not be gender-based but instead are related to the role taken by either parent.

Evaluation

Lamb (1981) suggested that different attachments simply serve different purposes rather than being in a hierarchy. Bowlby's (1969) view was that the different relationships are not equivalent. He claimed that in both the Scottish and Ganda samples most infants regularly showed more protest in a Strange-type Situation when one special person left them. This would suggest a special emotional relationship with this one person.

Summary

In this chapter we have looked at the attachment process, one of proximity-seeking and interaction. We examined the sequence of developmental events leading up to specific attachments, from asocial response to multiple attachments. The quality of an infant's attachments can be measured using the Strange Situation which shows whether a child is securely or insecurely attached in terms of separation and stranger anxiety, and exploration and reunion behaviours. The importance of such secure or insecure attachments lies in their short-term and long-term consequences for emotional (relationships) *and* cognitive development, as well as personality generally. The final issue which was looked at was the debate over whether secure attachments involve one (monotropy) or many people.

Review exercise

1 What is the importance of secure attachments, in the short and long term? Try to identify at least four outcomes.
2 Suggest at least two methodological and/or ethical criticisms of the empirical research described in this chapter.

Further reading

Bowlby, J. (1969) *Attachment and loss, volume 1: Attachment.* Harmondsworth: Penguin. The classic book in the field. It is useful to go right back to the source which describes many relevant studies and theories.

Meins, E. (1997) *Security of attachment and the social development of cognition.* Hove, Sussex: Psychology Press, Ltd. Full of interesting recent research, used to argue for a Vygotskian approach to attachment.

Shaffer, D.R. (1993) *Developmental psychology.* Pacific Grove, California: Brooks/Cole. A general textbook with a wealth of useful and interesting material. Chapter 11 is on early emotional development.

Smith, P.K. and Cowie, H. (1991) *Understanding children's development.* Oxford: Blackwell. Another general textbook on development with useful chapter on children's relationships with parents and families.

5

Privation

Introduction

The attachment process provides the developing child with a secure base for exploration and the foundation of later relationships. What happens when the attachment process fails? We have met the name Bowlby several times now and you may recall that he was the author of the most influential attachment theory. In his first version he called it 'the maternal deprivation hypothesis' because he focused on the purportedly catastrophic effects which occur when a child is deprived of maternal attachment. (Note that maternal does not necessarily equal mother, it refers to 'mothering' which can be done by anyone even a wolf as in the case of the legend of Romulus and Remus.)

Michael Rutter (1972, 1981) was basically supportive of Bowlby's theory but identified various flaws, one of which was that Bowlby had muddled together a variety of different kinds of deprivation. An infant or child can be *deprived* of a caregiver's presence, meaning that the child had formed attachment bonds but these were now disrupted, or the child can suffer from *privation*. It is the difference between having loved and lost, or simply never having loved or been loved.

Rutter said that the latter kind of loss, privation, would have very different consequences from deprivation. Furthermore, as regards deprivation, there can be short-term bond disruption as in day care arrangements, or long-term ones such as the death of a parent or some divorces.

We will examine the more common kinds of deprivation, or separation, in the next chapter. In this chapter we will discuss examples of privation. Despite the distinction between the terms 'deprivation' and 'privation', one ends up talking about being 'deprived' because the word 'privated' doesn't exist – but we can invent it!

Children reared in isolation

There are numerous stories, throughout history, of children who have spent their early years privated of human company and in conditions of utter neglect. Such tales capture our imagination and invoke feelings of painful incomprehension. Victor, the wild boy of Aveyron, and Kasper Hauser are cases which were given the Hollywood film treatment. Psychologists have written case histories of privated children discovered this century. Mason (1942) described Isabelle, child of a deaf mute mother who was found aged 6 locked in an attic. She was suffering from rickets, lacked speech and was seemingly unaware of relationships. With specialist help she made a rapid recovery both cognitively and emotionally, and at age 14 was showing very few developmental delays. Davis (1947) studied Anna, another child rescued from terrible conditions at the age of 6. She received no specialist help and made limited progress, dying when she was 10½. Clearly the outcomes can be very different.

The Koluchová twins (PM and JM)

Koluchová's (1972, 1976, 1991) study of these twin Czechoslovakian boys is one of the longest and most detailed records. Their mother died soon after they were born and they were fostered for the first 1½ years of their lives, finally being taken back by their father and a step-mother who treated them cruelly and locked them away in a cupboard. They were kept apart from the rest of the family and were deprived of proper food, exercise and stimulation. When they were rescued, at the age of 7, they reportedly looked like 3-year-olds and their speech was very limited. Fortunately for them, they were adopted by exceptionally caring sisters and made good progress, later marrying and having children. They are reported now to be stable and enjoying warm relationships.

Genie

The case of Genie (Rymer, 1993; Curtiss, 1977) demonstrate a less successful outcome. She was 13 when her mother sought help for her. Her father had locked her away because he thought she was retarded and vulnerable. He, in fact, committed suicide after Genie was discovered possibly because of his own guilt. Genie may have been retarded and this would explain her subsequent difficulties in acquiring language and making a full recovery. At the age of 13 she looked like a child half her age, and she was physically, emotionally and cognitively underdeveloped. Her recovery was hampered by an unsettled time with a variety of carers including one spell with foster parents who further abused her. One notable and autistic feature of her behaviour was that she showed a disinterest in other people, she didn't reject them but simply treated them in the same way as she treated inanimate objects.

Evaluation

Several conclusions can be reached from the study of these case histories. First, given adequate subsequent care children can recover. Second, age may be significant. One reason for Genie's lack of recovery might have been her advanced age when discovered. She may have been beyond the sensitive period for the development of emotional relationships and therefore could not have recovered even if her circumstances had been better. Third, the effects of early emotional and physical privation may be permanent.

However, any conclusions must be considered in light of the drawbacks of these studies. Most obviously it is not reasonable to make generalisations from individual case histories. It might be that these children were especially resilient or, on the other hand, they may have been congenitally retarded.

Second, we have no means of assessing the extent to which these children were without emotional relationships during their early years. The Czech twins had each other and there is evidence that peers can act as attachment figures. This was what Harlow found with the monkeys, as did Freud and Dann (1951) in the study of a group of children who had only each other during their early years in a concentration camp. Despite catastrophic early deprivation, these children went on to show good recovery, which was thought to be due to the peer support. Genie's mother also claimed to have had a relationship with her daughter even though Genie was locked up (Rymer, 1993).

Third, we cannot separate the effects of physical and emotional privation. It may be that poor psychological development can be explained, for example, in terms of poor nutrition and limited experiences of the world generally.

Finally, we should remember that the data collected may be unreliable because the early details were retrospectively recalled and based on interviews which may be biased.

Progress exercise

1 List three things that one (or more) of these studies tell us about the attachment process.
2 Select two of the case histories presented here and suggest one similarity and one difference in terms of the children's experiences and later recovery.

Institutionalisation

Another line of evidence has come from larger-scale studies of children reared in institutions for some or all of their early lives. Such institutions were places of extreme privation where children lacked cognitive and emotional stimulation. The lack of close relationships was partly because of necessity but also partly because people were unaware of the potential long-term consequences for such children.

Skeels' study

The work conducted by Harold Skeels (see Chapter 1) suggested that even very basic emotional care can have a major positive effect on subsequent cognitive development. Skeels and Dye (1939) recorded a case history of two apparently retarded children who, when transferred from an orphanage to a home for mentally retarded women, showed significant **IQ** gains. It was suggested that the extra attention they were given by the inmates resulted in the formation of attachments and facilitated their cognitive development.

On the basis of this, Skodak and Skeels (1949) conducted an experiment with orphanage inmates. Thirteen infants aged between 11 and 21 months were transferred to a home for the mentally retarded while a control group remained in the orphanage. After 1½ years the IQs of the control group fell from an average of 87 to 61 points whereas the transferred group's IQ rose from 64 to 92 points. Skeels (1966) assessed the children twenty years later and claimed that the effects were still apparent.

It has been suggested that one reason for these substantial differences could be that the researchers expected the transferred group to do better and the children were positively affected by these expectations, leading them to do better.

Bowlby's early view was that a 'bad' (psychologically impoverished) home was preferable to an institution because institutions 'convert a physically neglected but psychologically well-provided child into a physically well-provided but emotionally starved one' (Bowlby *et al.*, 1952). To some extent Skeels' research supported this because it suggested that any attention is better than none at all since it means that a child can form some attachments.

Tizard's study

Barbara Tizard directed a longitudinal study of 65 children who had been placed in an institution when they were less than 4 months old. There was an explicit policy in the institution against caregivers forming attachments with the children and, before the age of 4, the children had had an average of 50 different caregivers. This would suggest that the children (and the caregivers) were unlikely to have formed any specific attachments and indeed, they were described at age 2 as running to greet anyone who entered the room and yet they were more fearful of strangers than the control sample of children raised by their natural parents without experiencing any separations.

Progress exercise

What behaviours would you associate with secure or insecure attachment?

By the age of 4, twenty-four of the institutionalised children had been adopted, fifteen had returned to their natural homes and the rest remained in the institution. The study also included the control group of children described above. This natural experiment allowed the researchers to examine the effects of early deprivation on later development and compare the effects of the children's different attachment experiences. The children were assessed at age 4, 8 and 16 (Tizard and Rees, 1975; Tizard and Hodges, 1978; Hodges and Tizard, 1989).

Hodges and Tizard (1989) detected the following trend by age 16: the adopted children generally had close attachments to their parents and good family relationships whereas this was much less true for the children who had been restored to their homes. The latter group had often returned to the same difficult circumstances which had precipitated the need for care in the first place, and to parents who may have felt ambivalent about them. In contrast, adopted children went to homes where the parents had very much wanted a child.

The conclusion was that there were differences between the two ex-institution groups, adopted and restored, *within* their family relationships. However there were similarities in the behaviour of the two groups *outside* the family, when interacting with other adults and peers. Both groups were more likely to seek adult attention and approval than the control children, and were less successful in peer relationships.

Therefore the early effects of institutionalisation were seen to be ameliorated by subsequent attachments but there were also lasting effects.

Those children who remained in the institution after the age of 4 were not followed, mainly because only one remained in an institution by the age of 16. In addition, information from this group could not have thrown any light on the effects of subsequent positive experiences.

Evaluation of Tizard's study

Two points to consider in relation to this study are (1) there were considerable individual differences within each group suggesting that there are numerous factors at work, not simply attachment experiences, and (2) not all children were followed through the whole study (only forty-two were left at the end), those who 'dropped out' may have biased the final sample. For example, Hodges and Tizard reported that adopted children who remained in the study had fewer adjustment problems at age 4 whereas the restored children who remained in the study had earlier shown somewhat more adjustment problems than those who dropped out. In other words, the restored children who were less well adjusted were the ones who tended to drop out leaving a 'better' sample of restored children.

In addition some of the adopted children who remained in the study had been adopted after the age of 4 and one of them had spent time in a psychiatric institution, all of which highlights the lack of homogeneity of the group.

Finally, we might also consider the fact that the adoptive homes were often more affluent and the parents more educated than the families of the 'restored' children.

Other studies

The conclusions reached by Hodges and Tizard are supported by a number of other studies.

Pringle and Bossio (1960) looked at the adjustment of children living in an institution, identifying two groups: those who were stable and those who were maladjusted. They found that the former children tended to be those who maintained contact with their parents or parent substitutes, whereas only one of the maladjusted children did.

They also reported that the maladjusted children seemed unable to form lasting relationships with other adults or their peers. This suggests that it is the disruption or lack of attachments which is fundamentally important to adjustment.

Triseliotis (1984) recorded the lives of 44 adults who had been late adopted and whose prognosis had been poor. These adults showed good adjustment which was attributed to the fact that they had escaped from severe privation to a good, caring environment.

Bohman and Sigvardsson (1979) found that where institution-alised children were returned to their biological mothers even the length of their institutional stay appeared to have no effect on subsequent school performance or adjustment. On the other hand, children who were adopted or fostered did appear to be affected by the length of their institutional stay insofar as those children who spent more than six months in the institution showed slightly lower performance and were less well adjusted than those who spent less than six months in the institution. The researchers suggested that these contradictory findings may reflect the fact that children who are adopted earlier tend to be the more likeable ones. Therefore, we might conclude that recovery is possible but other factors may intervene in the final outcome and make it appear as if institutionalisation had long-term effects.

Romanian orphans

Recently a number of researchers have been able once more to study the effects of severe privation because of access to institutions where young children are still being looked after in extremely poor circumstances.

Rutter *et al.* (1998) studied 111 Romanian orphans adopted in the UK before the age of 2. On arrival these children were severely developmentally impaired, for example they were below the 3rd percentile for weight and head circumference (i.e. less than 3 per cent of children in their age group shared the same low measurements). In contrast, a control group of English adoptees showed none of these delays. By the age of 4 Rutter *et al.* reported that the Romanian children had caught up spectacularly, however the age at adoption was negatively correlated with attainment of developmental milestones by the age of 4. In other words the later the children were adopted, the slower their progress. We will have to await future reports to see if the later adoptees do eventually catch up.

Another study of Romanian orphans by Morison *et al.* (1995) compared two groups of age and sex-matched orphans. One group spent at least eight months in a Romanian orphanage before adoption whereas the others were adopted within four months. They found that the later adopted children made up many of the delays they initially showed and were progressing at a rate of two developmental quotient (which is similar to IQ and based on a test of developmental milestones) points per month in adoptive homes.

On the other hand, Dennis's (1960) study of orphans in the Lebanon found that children who were adopted after the age of 2 appeared unable to catch up intellectually with their peers. It may be that, in this study, the children went to homes where conditions were not that much better than the orphanages, at least in terms of intellectual stimulation.

Conclusions

One of the main issues in Bowlby's argument was that the lack of an attachment figure in early infancy should lead to permanent emotional maladjustment and relationship difficulties later in life. The studies of what happens to institutionalised children who *lacked* early attachments appears to undermine this argument. They indicate that, as long as children subsequently experience good attachments, they are likely to recover reasonably well.

I say 'reasonably well' because, as we have seen, there appear to be some differences between ex-institutional children and their more normal peers. Clarke and Clarke (1979) put forward a transactional model to explain this. It may be that the adopted children in the Hodges and Tizard study got on well within their families because the families made special efforts to love them, whereas they did not experience this outside the home and thus were unable to form relationships as easily or well. This would suggest that the children's ability to form relationships *was* affected by their early privation, and reminds us of the reciprocal nature of relationships. Children may cope as long as the other partner is able and/or willing to make special efforts but when they are on a level playing field (with others who are not making special efforts) their early experiences may cause difficulties.

One final point, worth mentioning, is that little account is taken of the peer support that institutionalised children may have experienced. After all, Freud and Dann (1951) suggested that these peer attachments enabled their concentration camp children to survive emotionally.

Progress exercise

List three possible conclusions which could be drawn from the studies of institutionalised children.

Reactive attachment disorder

Some children who experience early disruptions in the attachment process *do* appear to be *unable* to recover, as in children suffering from **reactive attachment disorder**. The symptoms are: lack of ability to give and receive affection, cruelty to others especially pets, abnormalities in eye contact and speech patterns, lying and stealing, lack of long-term friends, and extreme control problems. The diagnosis is only made when there are no other likely causes for the lack of social responsiveness, such as mental retardation (Parker and Forrest, 1993).

It is suggested that the cause of the disorder is a lack of primary attachments due to early maternal rejection and separation. For example, one typical case history described a young boy whose mother had not wanted him and put him up for adoption. This was followed by a series of foster homes until he was finally adopted at age 18 months. However he appeared unable to accept the affection his adopted parents tried to give him and, as an older child, engaged in lying, stealing, sending death threats and going into wild rages (Flanagan, 1996).

Children with attachment disorder are often those who have experienced multiple foster homes and late adoptions. Maternal rejection can occur even when the mother remains present and may be linked to one particular kind of child abuse. Jones *et al.* (1987) described some mothers as 'primary rejectors'. These tend to be middle class women who have had an unwanted child, a difficult pregnancy and/or experienced early separation from their infant due to problems at the time of birth. The mothers may well have good relationships with other children and are able to offer a good standard of physical care. Rejection starts from the time of birth and the mother–infant relationship never recovers. Gradually the guilt and lack of empathy that the mother feels turns into anger and, later in childhood, a period of stress or naughtiness may result in excessive punishment and abuse. In fact Lynch and Roberts (1982) suggested that bonding failure may be a key feature in *all* abusive relationships.

The advantage of making a diagnosis of attachment disorder is that it can lead to appropriate preventive and interventive action in terms of therapy for both parents and their children.

The effects of privation

The chief effect of privation is the effect on the individual's potential to form subsequent relationships, but there are many other, related short-term effects:

- *Affectionless psychopathy*. Bowlby used this term to describe the behaviour of the young delinquents he studied (see key research summaries on p. 133). He suggested that they displayed a lack of normal affection, shame or sense of responsibility and were unable to form permanent and emotionally meaningful relationships. In some ways their behaviour is rather similar to that described for children suffering from reactive attachment disorder.
- *Anaclitic depression*. Spitz (1945) used this term to describe the severe and progressive depression found in institutionalised infants which resulted from a lack of attachments. Subsequent research has found similar reactions in other primates (e.g. Hogg *et al.*, 1994; also see p. 33).
- *Reduced immune response*. Spitz also noted that the children who remained in institutions were prone to becoming ill despite a good standard of physical care. There may be some association between

the stress of emotional deprivation and physical illness. For example, Kiecolt-Glaser *et al.* (1984) found evidence of reduced immune responses in students who were experiencing stress.

* *Deprivation dwarfism.* Widdowson (1951) studied a group of apparently malnourished orphanage children. Despite being given dietary supplements they remained underdeveloped. However, when a new supervisor arrived who gave them better emotional care they began to improve. Many of the studies mentioned in this chapter, of children reared in isolation or in institutions, have found significant physical underdevelopment. It is likely that the hormones produced by stress affect growth as well as physical health to produce this 'deprivation dwarfism'.

Some conclusions

Clarke and Clarke (1998) point out that for most people, early experience represents 'no more than an initial step on the ongoing path of life'. In other words, for most people early experience is very much related to what happens later on. Bad experiences are likely to be followed by more of the same. However, where severely bad experiences are followed by much better ones the prognosis is *likely* to be good. Where a child remains in a continuing poor environment the early experience is merely compounded. Early experience matters but is not irreversible. However, we must remember that relationships are a two-way process, so that the child who suffers early privation may become quite hard to love, as in reactive attachment disorder.

There are a few specific issues we should consider.

Privation or deprivation?

It is hard to know, in the research discussed in this chapter, whether the children *never* formed any specific attachments or whether the attachments were 'simply' rather poor ones. The other factor to bear in mind is that many of the children were deprived in general cognitive terms not just emotionally. For example, institutionalised infants often spent days in cots where they received very little stimulation of any sort. This alone might account for their developmental delays, both cognitive and emotional.

A sensitive period?

Bowlby (1951) initially suggested that good mothering was almost useless if it was delayed beyond the age of 2½, though he later (Bowlby *et al.*, 1956) felt this had been too strong a claim. The evidence in this chapter certainly suggests that the concept of a critical period at any age is probably wrong because it seems that children can and do recover, given the right circumstances. It may be that there is a sensitive period and that at least some children are very susceptible to disruption during this time, for example those who suffer from reactive attachment disorder.

The concept of a sensitive period not only suggests special sensitivity at this time but also that attachments form most easily at this age because the individual is particularly receptive *and* is exhibiting behaviours which invite reciprocal attachments from caregivers. It is easier to come to love a small child than a more awkward and vociferous 5-year-old. More conscious effort is needed to form attachments beyond the sensitive period.

Individual differences in coping

As with any human characteristic the range of possible individual differences means that, in reality, generalisations are always inadequate. Some children require very little emotional support whereas others have a much greater need. Some people become entirely adequate adults despite having no close early emotional relationships. In addition we should remember that, in some societies, there is less emphasis on interpersonal relationships so that the kind of attachments discussed in this chapter may well not be universal for all people. This is discussed in Chapter 7.

Methodology

Research in this field is hampered by the obvious objections of subjecting children to deprived conditions. Therefore we have relied on situations where such conditions occur naturally. There are problems with this kind of research, in methodological terms, because they are not true experiments inasmuch as we have not *controlled* the independent variable and therefore conclusions about cause and effect are not entirely justified.

What does it matter?

The importance of this research, and the conclusions, is that it has warned people to take greater care when isolating young children and disrupting their attachments, for example in hospitals. However, Clarke and Clarke warn that there is a danger in this. The research may lead people to have lowered expectations for children who have suffered damage and this could affect such children's future.

Summary

Psychological research has looked at situations where children have suffered extreme early privation, such as case histories of children reared in isolation, studies of children living in institutions or those who have been adopted, and reactive attachment disorder. The possible effects of privation include: poor relationships with peers and adults, anaclictic depression or affectionless psychopathy and poor physical and cognitive development.

It seems that recovery is possible given good subsequent psychological care at a young enough age. However privated children may still find difficulties coping in situations outside the caring family. One should remember that some apparently privated children have actually had the affection of peers during their early development and therefore were deprived rather than privated. Equally, one should not confuse physical with psychological deprivation/privation as a cause of poor subsequent development, nor should one forget individual differences in resilience.

All of this means we cannot predict the consequences of early privation in a simple fashion. We can be certain that it is not desirable but should expect that it can be ameliorated.

With reference to the studies described in this chapter, discuss the effects of privation on emotional development with reference to three empirical studies. ['Discuss' means that you should both describe and evaluate the material.]

Note: try to distinguish between short-term and long-term effects and infant–caregiver as distinct from caregiver–infant effects.

Review exercise

Further reading

Gross, R. (1999) *Key studies*, 3rd edition. London: Hodder and Stoughton. The original text of Hodges and Tizard's article is presented plus a useful discussion of this and other studies of other deprived children. The article also appears in the other editions of the book.

Rymer, R. (1993) *Genie: escape from a silent childhood*. London: Michael Joseph. Readable account of Genie's case history, mainly focused on her difficulties in acquiring language.

6

Separation

Introduction

In the last chapter we focused on cases of extreme privation, where children experienced a *lack* of attachments as distinct from a *loss* of them. In particular, we concentrated on the lack of attachments in the child's early development, a time of heightened sensitivity in both infant and caregiver.

In this chapter we will look at situations of separation (loss), also referred to as '**bond disruption**', and consider what effect these may have on the developing child. These are all instances of a child deprived of its main attachment object, whether for short or long term.

In some cases separation is unavoidable, such as when a child has to spend time in hospital. In such situations we can ask how we might lessen the effects of bond disruption. In other situations, separation or bond disruption is not inevitable, for example day care and divorce. In these cases we might ask whether a decision should be taken against separation or, again, how we might lessen the effects.

We will start by looking at the child's responses to separation.

Responses to separation

Separation anxiety

Formation of attachment bonds provides the infant with a sense of security but, simultaneously, means that the infant also experiences anxiety when separated from their caregiver. This separation anxiety is used in the Strange Situation as a measure of security of attachment (see p. 44). The purpose of the anxiety is to maintain physical proximity between caregiver and child.

There are three typical phases of such a response which occur over a prolonged period of time (Robertson and Bowlby, 1952):

1   *Separation protest.* A securely attached child first responds to its caregiver's departure with protest. The child cries and appears to be very distressed. They may be easily comforted but are nevertheless inwardly angry and fearful. It is a natural response to loss and may last for a few hours or a few days.
2   *Despair.* The outward signs of protest gradually disappear and the child appears calm if slightly apathetic. In other words their emotionality is suppressed. They no longer look for their caregiver and may accept care from someone else though in a passive manner. The child may seek self-comfort through, for example, thumb-sucking or rocking.
3   *Detachment.* If the situation continues for longer, the child may appear to be coping reasonably well. However, this is deceptive because it masks the child's possible inner turmoil and unhappiness. When the caregiver returns the child is likely to respond indifferently or even aversively.

The extent of the distress varies according to the initial security of attachment (as we have seen in the section on security of attachment) as well as individual temperamental differences and also experience. If a child is frequently left and then reunited with his or her caregiver they may be better at coping if they have learned that being left is reliably followed by reunion. If the child's life is generally settled and/or they are left in familiar surroundings with their own toys this too will lessen their anxiety.

One might also remember that the caregiver experiences separation anxiety, and that the same phases of distress are manifested throughout life in coping with loss, for example when coping with the death of a loved one.

If infant–caregiver separation continues for a prolonged period, the result is likely to be severe anaclitic depression, as we saw in the last chapter.

Criticisms of the PDD model

This protest–despair–detachment (**PDD model**) pattern has been questioned by Barrett (1997). The original formulation was based on studies of children being left in hospital (Robertson and Bowlby, 1952). Barrett examined the films of these children and claimed that the children's initial response to separation could be better described as a determined effort to cope rather than protest. The children did later show signs of strain and distress, as described by Bowlby.

Barrett suggested a more complex account related to the original type of attachment between infant and caregiver. For example, a securely attached child may show little initial protest and cope relatively well whereas an ambivalent or avoidant child would be plunged more immediately into protest and despair and become quite disoriented.

This version has the advantage of taking individual differences into account and including the active role of the child and interactive nature of the relationship. It has the disadvantage of possibly being over-complex and leading to an under-estimation of the effects of separation.

Hospitalisation

One of the major influences on Bowlby's early thinking was those observations he made with James Robertson of children left in hospital or residential nurseries. The reaction of other psychologists to this film was that, even if the anxiety was due to the loss of the

Identify one short-term and one long-term effect of separation.

attachment figure, this could be easily overcome by the provision of good physical care. Robertson and Bowlby (1952) felt otherwise. They proposed that the separation was not so easily overcome, and in fact that it might easily lead to an extreme and pathological reaction.

The films made by Robertson with his wife (Robertson, 1952, Robertson and Robertson, 1967–73) showed that a key element to reducing the stress experienced during separation, and enabling speedy emotional recovery, was to minimise *bond disruption*. The Robertsons did this in one case by meeting the children beforehand with their parents and allowing the children to bring their own things with them when they came to stay with the Robertsons while their mother went into hospital. In another film, some children who were fostered while their mother had a baby in hospital were taken by the Robertsons to visit their mother (despite strong objections from the hospital) and clearly benefited afterwards though they cried when they saw her. On the other hand, they also filmed a cheerful and affectionate 18-month-old boy who was taken into residential care for nine days and shown becoming progressively more withdrawn and despairing. On return home he was sullen, rejected his mother, and there were severe behaviour problems throughout his childhood including repeatedly running away from home.

These were very strong images but, as they are case studies, it is difficult to make generalisations. It is also difficult to separate the trauma of being ill, or stress of having a new sibling, from the effects of bond disruption. Nevertheless, the work of the Robertsons and Bowlby had a profound effect on hospital policies, promoting the view that more attention needed to be paid to emotional rather than simply physical care. In particular, it became generally accepted that parents and children should be allowed unrestricted visiting when either are in hospital to avoid the consequences of bond disruption.

Hospitals and later maladjustment

Hospitals were also the focus of Spitz and Wolf's (1946) study, described on p. 3. They observed how apparently normal children became seriously depressed after staying in hospital, though the children generally recovered well if the separation lasted less than three months. Longer separations were rarely associated with complete recovery.

Douglas (1975) analysed a vast amount of data gleaned from the National Survey of Health and Development, a longitudinal study of 5,000 children born during one week in 1946. The children were assessed at regular intervals up to the age of 26. Douglas found that children who had spent more than a week in hospital or had experienced repeated admissions under the age of 4, were more likely to have behaviour problems in adolescence and to be poor readers. Quinton and Rutter (1976) also found that repeated hospital admissions were associated with later problems whereas children admitted only once rarely had later difficulties.

However, Clarke and Clarke (1976) suggested that this apparent relationship may be due to a third factor, namely general home problems. In other words, children from disadvantaged homes were more likely to need hospital treatment and also more likely to have problems in adolescence. The cause of difficulty was suggested to be the home background rather than the separation.

Further support for the view that hospital separation does not always lead to maladjustment came from a naturalistic study conducted by Bowlby et al. (1956). They studied 60 children who had TB and spent between five and twenty-four months in a sanatorium outside London. The children were under the age of 4 when they were first hospitalised. The nursing system did not provide substitute mothering for the children but many of the children were visited weekly by their families (i.e. bond disruption was minimised). When the TB children were assessed later by their teachers and a psychologist, it was found that there were very few differences between them and their school peers in terms of later intellectual development and emotional adjustment. Therefore, it would appear that hospitalisation does not inevitably have harmful effects possibly as long as bond disruption is minimised.

Evaluation

Studies of children in hospital are similar to those of institutionalised children – there are a variety of factors which may be causing distress aside from separation. Receiving treatment in hospital and being ill are likely in themselves to provoke anxiety, aside from any bond disruption. Kirkby and Whelan (1996) concluded after a review of recent research that there are a range of variables that influence the extent of a child's negative reactions to hospitalisation, which include the family's previous medical experience, the child's developmental status, the quality of the parent–child interaction, the seriousness of the illness, the severity of the medical procedure, and the coping style adopted by a child.

It is likely to be the constellation of anxiety-provoking factors which cause distress. However, it is precisely at such moments that children most need their attachment figures to reduce their sense of anxiety and therefore the distress is likely to be exacerbated when a child is separated from his or her main source of comfort. The children in the TB sanatorium may have felt less distressed at the *reason* for their hospitalisation and therefore been less affected by the disruption of attachment bonds.

The fact that they maintained family contacts was also important, which leads us to the conclusion that it is probably not separation which is important but rather it is the bond disruption which matters. Where children are allowed to maintain contact with attachment figures the ill-effects of separation seem to be considerably reduced.

We should also bear individual differences in mind. Those children who are more securely attached will cope better than those who aren't, as Barrett suggested.

Progress exercise

A 5-year-old child called Mary has to spend a month in hospital for a series of operations to correct a heart defect. Her parents are concerned that she will be unhappy but cannot take time off work to be with her. Suggest two (or more) ways that the hospital staff might ensure that Mary's psychological distress is minimised during her stay.

Day care

We almost take it for granted today that local communities should be equipped with good preschool day-care facilities. However, psychologists have not always promoted this idea. One of the major issues raised by Bowlby's maternal deprivation hypothesis was the potentially *detrimental* effect of day care. In fact Bowlby did not specifically suggest that women should stay at home to look after their children but his readership took the message that, if absent mothers create unhappy children, then mothers need to be present full time. It is even possible that Bowlby's views were popularised by the post-war government to encourage a cheaper alternative to providing universal child care facilities. Bowlby's arguments could be alternatively interpreted as favouring *improved* child care where the child's emotional needs were placed foremost.

Whichever view one takes, the reality is that for some families there is little choice about whether one parent can afford to stay home, especially in single-parent homes. It is also the case that many parents actually want to work, for example for their own self-esteem.

Kagan *et al.* (1980) launched a large-scale study of day care arguing that a dual standard had grown up in the US during the late 1960s. The view was that lower-class children might benefit from day care as a source of intellectual enrichment (see, for example, the Headstart project described in Chapter 9). However this overlooked the potential ill effects of separation from attachment figures. So, Kagan *et al.* asked, was day care a poor substitute for being with one's mother (or other attachment figure)?

Day care in a nursery

Kagan *et al.* investigated this in a study where they set up a daycare centre in Boston, catering for middle- and lower-class families from various ethnic groups. The staff at the school each had special responsibility for a small group of children, thus ensuring close emotional contact. The study focused on 33 infants who attended the nursery full time from the age of 3½ months, and compared them with a matched home control group. The children were assessed during the following two years in terms of their attachments and cognitive achievements as well as general sociability. Kagan *et al.* found no consistently large differences between the two groups of children. There was large variability among all the children, but it was not related to the form of care.

1 Why do you think it important for the staff in day care to be emotionally involved with the children?
2 What research method(s) was used in this study?

Other studies have reported similar findings. Roopnarine and Lamb (1980) again studied American children and found no adverse effects from day care on psychosocial development. Andersson (1996) studied 128 Swedish children who had attended day care, and assessed them at age 13. The main finding was that all children, but especially boys, benefited from day care in terms of school achievement, in particular if they started before the age of 1 year. The Oxford Pre-school Project (Garland and White, 1980) also found positive effects of day care, namely that children in nursery schools were more active, competitive and assertive than those not in nursery.

On the other hand, Tizard (1979) found evidence that, irrespective of social class, the conversations between mother and child were more complex than between nursery teacher and child. Teachers had fewer exchanges and elicited less from the children, which may be due to the teacher's inevitably divided attention and less intimate relationship with the child. Such differences in conversation may well affect cognitive progress.

The benefits of day care, then, may be especially in terms of social and cognitive development but it seems not at an emotional cost. Clarke-Stewart *et al.* (1994) investigated the relationship between time spent in day care and quality of attachment in over 500 children. She found that 15-month-old children who experienced 'high-intensity' child care (thirty hours or more a week from age 3 months) were equally distressed when separated from their mothers in the **Strange**

Situation as 'low-intensity' children (less than ten hours a week). This suggests that attachment was not affected by the experiences of separation.

Day care with a childminder

One should remember that there are different *kinds* of day care. Some people feel that using a childminder, who looks after children in her own home, is preferable because it is more like being at home and therefore more likely to be emotionally satisfying for the child.

Mayall and Petrie (1983) studied a group of London children aged under 2 and their mothers and childminders. They found that the quality of care varied considerably. In situations where children were not thriving, the researchers found that the childminded children often spent the day in a under-stimulated environment, lacking love and attention. In other situations, poor adjustment could be attributed to problems in the children's own home. Mayall and Petrie concluded that the things which moderate the effects of child-care arrangements are the quality of the care, the stability of the arrangement, and the original attachment bond.

Another study which was part of the Oxford Pre-school Project (Bryant *et al.*, 1980) examined the quality of care provided by childminders for nearly 100 children and found that at least a third of the children were 'failing to thrive' and some were actually disturbed. This may be because many minders appeared to feel that they did not have to form emotional bonds with the children nor did they have to stimulate them. In fact, on the contrary, minders rewarded quiet behaviour therefore encouraging passivity and under-stimulation. Bryant *et al.* concluded that 'minding is thought to be a good form of care because it approximates more closely to being at home, but this may be a government-sponsored myth because childminding is a cheap form of care'.

Attachment to day-care provider

Researchers have begun to look beyond the effects of bond disruption and the mother–infant attachment, to an equally important issue of the child's attachment to the day-care provider. Howes and Hamilton (1992) found that the attachments children form with their primary caregivers in the day-care environment is remarkably similar to the attachments they form with their mothers. However, secure attachments only occurred with 50 per cent of caregivers as opposed to 70 per cent of mothers. The lower rate of attachment probably reflects the lower quality and closeness of the caregiver relationship which is probably due to the fact that day-care assistants are less committed to the child, less attached and engage in less intense interactions. This emphasises the need for high-quality child care. Howes *et al.* (1998) found that a modest intervention programme which aimed at improving the caregiving practices of caregivers in child care did improve the attachment security of children within child care.

Evaluation

Mayall and Petrie (1983) concluded that day care need not be disruptive but it may be. Therefore it may be more desirable to focus on how to improve the quality of day care rather than to decide whether it is a good or bad thing.

We can also consider day care in terms of the *different* potential effects it may have on the developing child. These can be measured in terms of emotional, social and cognitive outcomes. Studies have certainly shown positive benefits in terms of socialisation and cognitive development, especially where a child may be deprived of social and cognitive stimulation at home.

However these separate effects must not be considered in isolation. If poor emotional adjustment occurs it is likely to affect cognitive development because the child's anxiety will dominate their activity. Added to this one always needs to consider the social and political climate of the time in which the research was conducted.

Progress exercise

Describe two conclusions which can be drawn from the studies of day care.

Divorce

The link between divorce and bond disruption is not necessarily clear. When parents separate or divorce, a child will stay with one parent and may have good contact with the other parent. So in what way is this disruptive? It was assumed, from Bowlby's initial analysis, that separations led to maladjustment. Indeed, there is evidence that children from divorced families have higher rates of delinquency in adolescence and greater emotional maladjustment. For example, Wallerstein and Kelly (1985) claimed that 80 per cent of children appearing in US psychiatric clinics came from broken homes.

However, Rutter (1972) suggested that there was a logical flaw in this argument. It could be that it was not separation *per se* which caused the maladjustment but the discord which accompanies, or even comes before, parents' decision to separate.

Parental discord

Cockett and Tripp (1994) compared the experiences of 152 children living in a variety of different families – single, divorced and intact. The children from different kinds of families were matched on key variables such as age, sex, mother's educational background, and socio-economic status. The study found that:

- Children from **reordered families** were more likely to have encountered health problems, experienced friendship difficulties and suffered from low self-esteem.
- Those children living in intact families, where there was marital discord, did less well than children whose parents rarely argued but they were better off than those from reordered families.

The conclusion must be that marital breakdown causes more problems for children than discord alone. However, the reordered families were also more likely to be receiving social security benefits, had moved house more often and were less likely to own their own car. Therefore, the differences between reordered and intact families might have been due to a variety of factors. There is one possible flaw in this. Where divorce has occurred the conflict prior to the divorce may have been more severe than where divorce was avoided.

81

Chess *et al.* (1984) looked at the effects of separation and divorce on 132 children whom they had followed from birth to early adulthood as part of the New York Longitudinal Study. Results indicated that parental conflict, especially regarding child management but including other issues, predicted poor adult adaptation. This was not the case where parents had separated without prior conflict.

There may be an interaction effect. Amato *et al.* (1995) conducted a twelve-year study of 2,033 married people, some of whom divorced over the course of the study. The researchers were able to interview nearly 500 adult offspring who had lived in the same household as the parents at the time of the initial interviews. They found that:

- In high-conflict families, the young adults were coping better if their parents divorced than if they stayed together.
- In low-conflict families, the young adults coped better if their parents stayed together than if they divorced.

This appears to suggest that conflict is worse than divorce, but where there is low conflict it is better for parents to remain together.

Explanations

The maladjustment which is associated with divorce may well be due to interparental conflict, as Rutter proposed. It may also be due to separation from one parent and the disruption of these attachment bonds, as Bowlby's theory suggested. However, the fact that delinquency is associated with divorce and not parental death suggests that this explanation is not sufficient (Holmes, 1993). A third possibility is the number of stressful life changes and economic hardships which accompany separation and divorce, as Cockett and Tripp's study found. Amato (1993) suggested that a further possibility is that the psychological adjustment of parents will influence the bonds with the child and the child's ability to cope.

Final evaluation of separation experiences

All of the experiences looked at in this chapter have inevitably been recounted in rather generalised terms. This is in part because there is a lack of homogeneity in the experiences being described. To say that a child comes from a divorced family or attends day care only very approximately describes the child's experience and it is a gross over-simplification of the experience and associated problems.

Ainsworth (1972), in a review of research on separation, concluded that there did appear to be a slight increase in later psychological disturbance in children who were separated from their parents for more than a month during their early years. However, she felt that it was difficult to see how such short separations might have such large consequences. Instead it was likely that children who experience separations also have to cope with multiple problems associated with the separation, such as family distress or conflict prior to divorce, and it is the constellation of problems which leads to long-term effects. Good attachment bonds with one or several other people would help the child to cope.

Summary

In this chapter we have considered children's responses to separation in terms of the PDD model and the likelihood that individual differences should be taken into account. We considered the effects of separation in the context of hospitalisation, day care and divorce. The conclusions have been that each of these experiences can have undesirable outcomes but that there are important individual differences and it is not always clear that the *cause* of distress is due to separation. Distress may equally be due to associated conflict or tension. Children can cope as long as their 'psychological list' of problems is not too great.

The recommendation is that our attention should be focused on how to improve the quality of the child's attachment experiences within the context of separation, rather than seeking to blame or prevent separation.

Contrast the studies and conclusions from this chapter, with those from Chapter 5. List at least three differences that you can identify between the effects of privation and separation.

Review exercise

Further reading

Bee, H. (1995) *The developing child*. New York: HarperCollins. Developmental textbook which contains small sections on day care and divorce.

Robertson, J. (1958) *Young children in hospitals*. London: Tavistock Publications. An accessible, relatively brief book presenting views and case histories which helped change the hospital system.

Schaffer, H.R. (1998) *Making decisions about children*, second edition. An excellent resource containing summaries of lots of research articles especially related to issues such as divorce, but also generally to attachment.

7

Social and cultural variations

Introduction
Cultural variations in attachment
Cultural variations in childrearing
Conclusion
Summary

Introduction

The picture of early socialisation which has been presented so far has largely overlooked one critical factor. It only represents the approach of one culture to childrearing. The view of attachment applies mainly to a particular social group (middle-class parents), to a particular ethnic group (White Europeans) and to a particular historical period (the twentieth century). Why do I say this? Because much of the research has involved the behaviour and attitudes of White, middle-class Europeans and it is entirely from this century.

In this chapter we will consider some examples of what is similar and what is different across social and cultural groups. This will enable us to assess to what extent the attachment process is universal and innate, or to what extent it is strictly a cultural phenomenon. We might also note that cross-cultural research enables us to gain insights into our own cultural practices and to develop a less ethnocentric view of human behaviour.

What is 'cultural variation'?

The term 'culture' here refers to a set of rules, morals and methods of interaction that bind a group of people. These rules, morals and so on are the products of socialisation, that is we learn them through our social interactions with other members of our culture.

Within any culture there are 'sub-cultures'. We might consider that different social classes are in effect sub-cultures, and therefore can include class differences within the context of cultural variation.

We would expect the wider issue of childrearing to be related to culture and sub-culture because childrearing methods are the processes by which children are socialised. In contrast, we might think that the attachment process is less related to culture because of the proposed mechanisms which underlie attachment, such as the infant's innate propensity to elicit caregiver attention and for the caregiver to respond.

We will look at cross-cultural evidence related to attachment first and then at the evidence related to childrearing practices more generally.

Cultural variations in attachment

Cultural similarities

We have seen that infants first express separation anxiety around the age of 7 months. Konner (1981) reported that the same is true in virtually every culture at about the same age regardless of caregiver contact or other experiences. This is strong support for the biological determination of attachment.

Perhaps the differences are more noticeable in the way adult caregivers respond. For example, in Botswana adults hardly ever let a baby cry – babies are generally carried around by the mother and breastfed whenever they appear distressed (Konner, 1981).

The Strange Situation

The Strange Situation has been used by researchers in many different countries as a means of investigating attachment and/or making comparisons between cultures. Some of the evidence suggests that there are some cultural differences in the way that infants are attached. For example Nakagawa *et al.* (1992) tested Japanese infants aged less than 1 year and found that 75 per cent could be classed as secure whereas 21 per cent were in the resistant group. The remaining 4 per cent were unclassifiable. This suggests that there are more securely attached infants in Japan than in the UK (Campos *et al.*, 1983, if you recall, found 62 per cent secure).

Mizuta *et al.* (1996) studied Japanese and American children of 4 and 5 years and did not find differences in security of attachment though they did observe a greater desire for bodily closeness in the Japanese children.

Perhaps the most comprehensive analysis was presented by IJzendoorn and Kroonenberg (1988) who amalgamated the results from 32 studies conducted in eight different counties. Percentages of secure attachments ranged from 50 per cent in China to 75 per cent in Britain. Bee (1995) cautioned against over-interpreting this evidence because most of the studies were actually based on rather small samples.

The Strange Situation as an imposed etic

The term '**imposed etic**' describes the use of a technique developed in one culture to study another culture. An 'etic' is a universal behaviour as distinct from an 'emic', which is a culturally specific behaviour. An example would be 'phonetics' which is the study of sounds that people produce, as distinct from 'phonemics' which is the study of the way sounds are used to produce meaning in a particular culture.

The Strange Situation is an example of an imposed etic, as also are the intelligence tests designed by Western psychologists. The Strange Situation assumes that the behaviour of all children in all cultures means the same thing whereas this may be unjustified. Takahaski (1990) pointed out that, for example, in Japan children may be very distressed when they are left alone because in Japan children are never left alone. Therefore, in the Strange Situation, a Japanese child's anxiety might be due to the unusualness of the situation rather than the degree to which they are securely attached.

Having said this, the fact that IJzendoorn and Kroonenberg (1988) found a very similar figure for secure attachment for many cultures (between 64 and 68 per cent in the US, Japan, the Netherlands and Israel) suggests that they may be measuring something similar.

Indeed, Bee (1995) concluded that the same factors contribute to mother–infant interactions in all cultures.

One or many attachments?

A different kind of cross-cultural investigation has looked at the number of attachments that infants form. In an earlier chapter we considered whether infants do form one main attachment (monotropy) with a hierarchy of qualitatively lesser ones, or many equivalent ones. In our own society it would appear that one *primary* attachment is the rule, though as fathers spend increasingly more time with their infants this may be becoming less true. What about other cultures?

Thomas (1998) questions whether the tendency to form a single main attachment might in fact be maladaptive. It might be more desirable to have a network of attachments to sustain the needs of a growing infant who has a variety of demands for social and emotional interactions.

Ainsworth (1967) studied members of the Ganda tribe of Uganda where the pattern of child care involved multiple carers, and concluded that the infants nevertheless formed one primary attachment.

Tronick *et al.* (1992) studied a pygmy tribe, the Efe, from Zaire who live in extended family groups. Infants and children were looked after by whoever was closest to hand. They were breastfed by different women but usually slept with their own mother. Tronick *et al.* found that, by the age of 6 months, the infants still did show a preference for their mothers, a single primary attachment.

An older study by Fox (1977), described in the key research summaries in Chapter 10 (p. 137), looked at life in kibbutzim, a type of Israeli farming community where children spend most of their time with nurses called metapelets, but see their mothers for a few hours a day after work. When the children were placed in the Strange Situation they protested equally when either mother or metapelet left but were more comforted by their mothers at reunion. This would suggest a stronger or more secure attachment to the mother, supporting the idea that it is the *quality* of time spent together not the *quantity* that counts.

We should note that the metapelets had to divide their attention among many children and had less interest in any one individual, which would explain why the children were less attached. There was also one key flaw in this study, namely the fact that there was quite a high turnover rate of metapelets. Therefore the Strange Situation might be measuring duration (quantity) rather than strength of attachment after all. Where the metapelet is a more permanent figure, attachment might be stronger.

Are there any differences?

There appear to be a great many similarities but there are a few cross-cultural studies which have reported quite different early attachment styles. Mead's (1935) classic description of the Mundugumour tribe was one of active dislike of their offspring and lovelessness.

Similar observations were reported by Turnbull (1972) of the Ik, a Ugandan tribe with whom he lived for a while. He claimed that parents appeared to show outright dislike for their children from birth and the children were left to fend for themselves at the earliest opportunity. A key feature of Ik existence was that life was extremely impoverished and they lived on the brink of starvation.

Kagan and Klein (1973) also observed a society where young infants were raised in extreme privation. The villagers of a small Guatemalan community kept their infants indoors to protect them from dirt and disease. Kagan and Klein reported that the infants had almost no contact with people and lived in the darkness with no play objects. When they were assessed at the age of 1 they were very backward. When they were assessed again years later, after having had more 'normal' social and physical interactions, they performed at levels equivalent to Western children. This suggests that their early privation did not affect their cognitive development. However, the outward appearance of privation may not have been the case. They may well have had some limited contact with others when they were fed which may have enabled the development of attachment bonds.

These studies show us that attachment and caring are not found in all human societies and this suggests that it may therefore not be innate or 'fixed' behaviour.

Attachment and economics

Schaffer (1998) argued that the exceptions described above demonstrate that maternal love cannot be seen as an inevitable and universal part of human nature. It may be an innate *capacity* but one which is susceptible to environmental and cultural influences. He also pointed out that in Britain, even as little as 100 years ago, children were similarly treated with little empathy. In both instances we are considering societies which lack and lacked economic affluence. Therefore, one could argue that economics is the key to attachment. Societies may only be free to 'indulge' in rich infant–caregiver interactions when they are not restricted by the demands of work (mothers having to return to till the fields) or limited resources.

Alternatively, we can explain cultural differences in terms of the adult behaviours expected within a society. The childrearing methods used will prepare children for the appropriate emotional behaviour for that culture. Therefore, we would expect that children in an **individualistic society** would be brought up differently to those in a **collectivistic society**.

This could also explain the stark childrearing methods of the Mundugumour. The young were being socialised into being aggressive and warrior-like adults. Similarly the Ik's children needed to be prepared for the harsh realities of their life. Munroe and Munroe (1980) conducted a five-year study among the Logoli of Western Kenya, and concluded that infant care in this society was related to later emotional development. The children were given a great deal of attention, protection and indulgence which promoted the Logoli's benign view of life.

Conclusions

First of all, we can note that what infants do from their earliest moments may well be universal, yet they are very quickly socialised by the responses of other members of their culture. The responses made by adults to, for example, an infant's smile or cry may also be universal but they will also be very much a product of the adult's own socialisation experiences. The task of the caregiver is to turn the child into an integrated member of their culture. Hinde (1987) said that socialisation and acculturation go hand in hand.

Second, we should remember that we must be critical of the methods used by researchers when considering cross-cultural studies. As we have seen, it appears that the Strange Situation may be applicable across cultures. However when 'outsiders' record their observations of other societies, these observations may be affected by observer biases in the sense that it is difficult to interpret the practices of other societies without imposing one's own cultural expectations.

Third, we have seen that having one main attachment does seem to be the rule in all cultures, even where there is multiple caregiving.

Finally, we considered the view that, where there are cultural differences, these may be related to economics or prevailing conditions such as war. Alternatively differences may be understood in terms of preparing the child for different adult societies.

1 Describe one study which showed that 'normal' development does not appear to depend on attachments with others.
2 Suggest one criticism of this study (e.g. either the methodology or the conclusions).

Progress exercise

Cultural variations in childrearing

Studies of Western childrearing styles

Several studies have categorised childrearing styles and associated this with outcomes such as aggressiveness or moral behaviour. For example, Baumrind (1971) conducted many interviews and observations of parents and children, and identified three basic parenting styles which all assume parental involvement. A fourth style has been added for cases where there is little such involvement:

- *Authoritarian*. Adults impose rules on children, rarely explaining why the child should behave in a particular way but instead using punitive measures to ensure obedience. This is likely to result in a child who is achievement-oriented, prejudiced, moody, fearful, and/or passive.

- *Authoritative*. The adult uses a flexible approach, combining reason with clear guidelines and being responsive to the child's feelings. Children are typically self-reliant, self-controlled, cheerful, cooperative, and curious.
- *Permissive*. The adult leaves the child relatively free to express itself within fairly loose boundaries. Adults rarely exert control and are warm towards the child. This kind of parenting may result in rebelliousness, aimlessness, low achievement and a lack of self-control.
- *Rejecting–neglecting*. Caregivers are not involved with the child. They are uncontrolling, over-permissive and aloof, possibly because of their own problems. They may be actively rejecting or simply neglectful. This results in antisocial and rebellious children who are hostile.

Other psychologists, such as Hoffman (1970), have proposed similar schemes of parenting styles. Hoffman also found that authoritativeness (he called it 'induction' parenting) was positively associated with more mature moral development than other parenting styles.

Evaluation

One point to consider is that these studies were correlational. We cannot know whether a particular parenting style *causes* a type of behaviour, only that there is a relationship between the two. It may be that children who are morally less well developed or who are less self-controlled require more coercive forms of punishment. However there is evidence that parents use similar styles with all their children, which would suggest their parenting is a feature of their personality rather than a response to a particular child (Dunn *et al.*, 1986).

It may also be that there were other significant features of the parenting styles apart from the way that parents exert control. Erikson (1963) suggested that there are two main dimensions of parent–child relationships, which are parental warmth and parental control. Indeed, a study by Rosenhan (1970) found that children were more likely to behave altruistically if they had warm relations with their parents during their childhood.

Social class (sub-cultural) differences

Some studies have focused on class differences in childrearing methods. Maccoby (1980) concluded from a review of relevant studies that there were at least four main differences between lower SES (socio-economic status) parents and higher SES ones:

- *Obedience* Lower SES parents stress obedience and respect for authority whereas higher SES parents emphasise curiosity and independence.
- *Discipline* Lower SES parents are more authoritarian and tend to use power-assertive forms of discipline. Higher SES parents are more likely to be permissive or authoritative.
- *Language*. Higher SES parents use more complex language and talk more with their children.
- *Warmth*. Higher SES parents show more warmth and affection towards their children.

An interesting feature of this list is that there are similarities between low SES parenting and the less affluent societies we looked at in the first part of this chapter. This may suggest, again, that childrearing is a reflection of the care parents can afford to give and the harsh reality of the child's life ahead. For example, Harkness and Super (1992) suggested that obedience is a characteristic which is valued in poorer societies whereas in more affluent conditions, such as parts of America, parents value intelligence and inquisitiveness.

There have been other documented differences. For example, Jones *et al.* (1987) reported that lower SES mothers are significantly less likely to breastfeed (40 per cent) than higher SES mothers (60 per cent). Breastfeeding is positively related to intelligence and health.

One should remember that any generalisations, such as those above, represent averages and not individuals. There are many lower and higher SES families who behave quite differently from the descriptions above.

Cross-cultural studies

Whiting (1963; Whiting and Whiting 1975) conducted a number of cross-cultural studies which reported behaviour in six different cultures (the Philippines, Mexico, Kenya, India, Japan and the US). Minturn and Lambert (1964) analysed this data and concluded that the differences within each culture were at least as great as those between cultures.

Barry *et al.* (1957) identified six central dimensions of childrearing that they claimed were common to all societies: obedience, responsibility, nurturance (caring for other members of the society), achievement, self-reliance and general independence. They claimed that these could be reduced to a single dimension, namely 'pressure towards compliance' where obedience represents one end of the scale and self-assertion is at the other extreme. One can compare one society to another in terms of these dimensions. For example, Barry *et al.* found that in all societies girls were socialised more for compliance, and also that societies which were more agricultural tended to be altogether more compliant than hunter-gatherer societies.

Conclusion

Attachment is a dynamic concept which must be understood within the appropriate cultural context. By and large the function of attachment is the same across cultures, namely the provision of an emotional base from which we have a template for culturally appropriate relationships and for self-esteem.

There are a variety of successful ways to bring up a child. Childrearing methods are cultural phenomena and are related to the attitudes and necessities of each social group. This is **cultural relativism**.

Summary

Culture is passed on through the process of socialisation, most especially childrearing practices. There are some cultural differences and some cultural universals in attachment, such as the amount of attention given to children (a difference) and the attachment to a primary caregiver (a similarity). There are also sub-cultural differences, for example variations in childrearing practices according to social class.

To some extent these differences can be understood in terms of the conditions within which a culture exists and the ideals of the culture. When considering these conclusions we must remember the methodological problems involved in cross-cultural research, such as observer bias, as well as the constraints of correlational research.

List four pairs of cross-cultural studies, each pair should present opposing views of attachment or childrearing. Briefly describe and evaluate each study.

Essay: What can cross-cultural research tell us about our child-rearing practices?

Review exercise

Further reading

Berry, J.W. (1992) *Cross-cultural psychology*. Cambridge: Cambridge University Press. A useful resource book with a whole chapter dedicated to studies of childrearing.

Theories
of attachment

Introduction

Which comes first, theory or empirical data? Empirical data informs theory and theory generates empirical research. A theory is a *systematic* collection of empirical facts offered as an explanation for a phenomenon. We need some facts before constructing a theory and then we need to test the theory by generating hypotheses and collecting facts to test the hypotheses.

Bowlby's theory was his attempt to make sense of empirical data and theories from, for example, Spitz, Lorenz, Harlow and Robertson's research. Over a period of forty years he adapted his theory to accommodate new data.

Much of the empirical work discussed in this book was generated by Bowlby's theory. For example, researchers such as Ainsworth and Schaffer set out to test the propositions of Bowlby's theory and thereby validate the theory or suggest modifications.

It is arguable as to whether a chapter on theories of attachment belongs at the beginning or end of a book. I have chosen to place it here in order to pull everything together and to be able to assess the theory in the light of the empirical evidence we have now examined. So this chapter is both a revision of material already covered and an opportunity to assess the theory formally.

What is a theory of attachment?

A theory of attachment seeks to account for several things, such as:

- What are the *characteristics* of the child's main attachment figure? Why do children become attached to one person and not another? Is it because of the amount of time spent with a caregiver, or the question of who feeds them, or is it related to the responsiveness of the caregiver?
- What is the *function* of attachment, in the short and long term? What are the consequences of healthy (secure) and unhealthy (insecure) attachment? What happens to children whose attachments are less than good?

Attachment theory before Bowlby

Freudian theory

Freud suggested that very young infants derive their greatest satisfaction from oral gratification. This first phase of infant development was called the **oral stage**. During this period the infant is attracted to any person who gives them oral pleasure, most typically their mother. Freud believed that attachment occurs because one individual satisfies the infant's instinctual need for oral gratification. The infant's caregiver would thus become a love object and this first love would form the basis of all later attachments.

Freud believed that an infant may develop an unhealthy attachment if they are either deprived of food/and or oral satisfaction, or if they are over-indulged. Unhealthy attachments result in later fixations on the oral channel in an attempt to satisfy the unsatisfied needs. This may be expressed in behaviours such as smoking and pencil-chewing, or in terms of certain personality traits such as impatience or greediness.

One of the central ideas of Freud's psychodynamic personality theory was that *deprivation* had far-reaching effects. A child who is deprived of instinctual needs is forever wanting.

Behaviourist theory

Behaviourists also felt that it is the person who provides nourishment who becomes the main attachment figure. They argued that the caregiver becomes a **conditioned reinforcer**. The infant has an **instinctive** (reflex) response to being fed. He or she experiences pleasure, and comes to associate the caregiver with this pleasure. This feeling generalises to a sense of pleasure whenever the caregiver is near.

Evaluation of Freudian and behaviourist approaches

Both approaches would lead us to expect infants to become most attached to the person who feeds them. However, Harlow's experiments with monkeys (see p. 31) demonstrated that attachment was more related to interactive body contact than feeding. Schaffer and Emerson's study (p. 137) found no relationship between feeding practices and strength of attachment. They also found only a small association between time spent together and attachment, only one-third of the infants were attached most to the person who spent the greatest amount of time caring for them. Therefore, we can conclude that neither feeding nor time spent together is sufficient to create attachment.

One of the general criticisms of Freud's theory of personality is that it was based on the study of pathological behaviour in adults. Freud used the recollections of his disturbed patients to make inferences about how their early experiences may have caused their later difficulties. He further extrapolated from this abnormal behaviour to suggest how normal development proceeds – a flawed logic.

There are also many criticisms of behaviourism generally, such as it being mechanistic and reductionist. In other words behaviourism reduces complex behaviour to a set of over-simplified structures and processes. On the positive side, behaviourists didn't suggest that it was only feeding which acted as a reinforcer but that it was a constellation of comforts such as being cuddled and caressed, stimulated and just generally cared for. So to some extent their account was 'correct'.

However, the theory of conditioning emphasised the infant's passive role, which is not supported by the evidence (see Chapter 2).

The ethological approach

The ethologists introduced the concept of imprinting to the attachment process. They believed that animals are born with innate drives that increase their survival potential. One of these drives is the predisposition to imprint upon a certain type of object (ones that make a certain noise or who move about) and this imprint tends to ensure that they stay close to a caregiver.

An imprint need not be simply visual. It may be related to smell, as in the case of goats or sound as in ducks. And it is something learned by both caregiver and offspring. One way to get a mother sheep whose own infant has died to adopt another orphan lamb is to wrap the lamb in the skin of the mother's dead lamb. This is because she has imprinted on the smell. There is good evidence that human infants also learn early to recognise their own mother's smell. For example, Cernoch and Porter (1985) demonstrated that infants of 12 days old can differentiate and prefer the underarm odour of their mother to a stranger, as long as the infants were breastfed.

Imprints have long-term as well as short-term consequences, most notably in terms of identifying an appropriate mate (see p. 29).

Bowlby's theory

There are four important points to consider in relation to Bowlby's theory:

- There were two main influences on his theory: psychoanalysis (the effects of deprivation) and ethology (the innateness and adaptiveness of attachment behaviours).
- There are two versions of his theory: the maternal deprivation hypothesis of the early 1950s and attachment theory which was presented in detail by the end of the 1960s.
- Attachment theory described how *both* infant and caregiver are innately programmed to form attachments: the infant has innate behaviours which elicit caregiving and the caregiver is innately programmed to respond.

- The theory emphasised both the *positive* consequences of attachment and the *negative* consequences of loss or lack.

The influence of psychoanalysis: maternal deprivation

The Freudian concept of deprivation shaped Bowlby's early thinking as he was a trained psychoanalyst. However, in his theorising he substituted maternal for oral deprivation. As a psychiatrist, his early focus was on the potentially pathological outcome of deprivation, in other words he was looking at severe depression and psychopathy.

The theory of maternal deprivation first appeared in 1951 in a book called *Maternal care and mental health* (which was republished in a popular edition as *Child care and the growth of love*, 1953). The central hypothesis was that maternal care was as necessary for healthy development as vitamins. Bowlby proposed that children who were deprived of early attachment would fail to thrive. Even more, he proposed that their mental health would suffer and they were likely to display affectionless psychopathy. Note that the term 'maternal' referred to 'mothering' rather than the mother. Bowlby never suggested that a maternal person had to be the child's mother.

Ultimately, Bowlby felt that the Freudian approach could not provide a full explanation for 'normal' behaviour.

The influence of ethology: attachment theory

Ainsworth (1982) reported that the concept of attachment came to Bowlby in a flash in 1952 when he first heard about the work of ethologists such as Lorenz and Tinbergen. By this time he had already spent time doing his own research on infant separation (see 'Forty-four thieves' in the key research summaries in Chapter 10 (p. 133).

The ethological perspective was, and is, based on the biological principles of evolution. All behaviours can be understood and explained in terms of their function for the individual, most notably the function of increasing survival. The function of attachment behaviours is to protect the infant and promote the survival of the gene pool and species. To be successful, attachment behaviours must be mutual, they must be present in both the infant and caregiver. Each participant triggers instinctual social behaviours in the other and both participants form an attachment relationship. This occurs through an innate set of social releasers: infants display certain behaviours (for example smiling and crying) and adults respond to them, for example by picking them up.

A critical or sensitive period

If the system is innate, then it must be biologically driven. Biological systems tend to have a 'window' of development. For example, if the visual system is deprived of stimulation it eventually becomes incapable of working properly. Early exposure to light and pattern is a requirement for normal development of the visual system (see Blakemore and Cooper's research which is discussed on p. 113). In terms of embryonic development this has been referred to as a critical period. In Chapter 3, we have seen that, in psychology, the concept of a 'sensitive period' is preferred.

Bowlby suggested that there is a sensitive period in the development of attachment, which occurs before the age of about 2½. After this age he felt that a child would no longer be capable of forming strong attachments and also that any disruption to attachment bonds during this sensitive period would have serious and irreversible long-term consequences.

Is attachment innate?

If attachment behaviour is innate, as the ethological view suggests, then we would expect it to be universal. Cross-cultural research (see Chapter 7) in general supports this in showing that infants do appear to form a primary attachment in all cultures. But there are exceptions, and there are cultural variations in the way that people in different cultures relate to their infants. Therefore we might conclude that *aspects* of attachment are innate.

Monotropy

In the early version of attachment theory, Bowlby introduced the term 'monotropy' to describe the fact that the child had one primary attachment figure (see p. 51). Bowlby always maintained that the child had many different attachments but they were not equivalents of each other. They formed a hierarchy with the maternal or primary caregiver at the top.

The importance of the primary caregiver lies in the model this provides for all subsequent relationships. It is this attachment, above all others, which has important and long-term emotional consequences. The mechanism by which this takes place is through the **internal working model**.

The internal working model

The internal working model is a set of conscious and/or unconscious rules and expectations regarding our relationships with others. This model develops out of the primary attachment relationship and is what it sounds like, a model or **schema** which is used as the template for future relationships.

Through this first emotional relationship the child is able to build up a set of models of themselves and of others. The securely attached child should have a positive picture of themselves and will be able to bring this to other relationships. The insecurely attached child sees themselves as unworthy of love and is therefore reluctant to enter into relationships.

One difficulty with this concept is the fact that it is hard to test empirically.

Caregiver sensitivity hypothesis

Holmes (1993) called Mary Ainsworth the 'co-founder of attachment theory' in her work with Bowlby. Her research provided the tool (the Strange Situation) for investigating secure and insecure attachments and led her to look at the features of the caregiver's behaviour which maximise secure attachment. She found that infants who receive warm, sensitive care become securely attached and that secure attachment does not create dependency, instead it enables independence – a key distinction between the Freudian approach which emphasised dependency and Bowlby's view that attachment created independence. This is the **caregiver sensitivity hypothesis**. An example of the empirical support for this can be seen in research by Bell and Ainsworth (1972) who studied twenty-six middle-class, white infant–mother pairs from soon after the infants were born. At the age of 1 the infants who cried least were the ones whose mothers had responded most promptly to their crying, suggesting a link between caregiver sensitivity and infant security. Schaffer and Emerson (1964) had also found that maternal responsiveness and total amount of stimulation were positively related to the infant's strength of attachment.

One interesting point to consider is that the extent of adult responsiveness is not universal. Some cultures, as we have seen, do not respond to their infants whereas others respond much more than we do.

A secure base

Another important effect of attachment is the effect it has on cognitive development. Exploration of one's environment is critical for such development and such exploration depends on a secure attachment. Ainsworth (1982) introduced the phrase 'secure base' to describe the way a child uses his attachment figure(s) as the pivot for their roving. They often return periodically to 'touch base'. An insecurely attached child is less willing to wander (see p. 45).

A related feature of exploration is the question of who initiates the separation. Children who initiate separation are more content to wander than a child who is left involuntarily on his own (Rheingold and Eckerman, 1970).

Progress exercise

1 Without looking back, list four key features of Bowlby's theory.
2 Identify at least one way in which Bowlby's account differed from early behaviourist theory, and one way in which they were the same.

Attachment theory

Hinde (1982) distinguished three interrelated concepts in Bowlby's attachment theory:

1 *Attachment*. This is the psychodynamic component of the theory. To be securely attached is to feel safe and secure. Insecure attachment leads to dependency.
2 *Attachment behaviour*. This is the behavioural component. Feelings of attachment result in the maintenance of proximity. Holmes (1993) called it a 'spatial theory' because attachments dictate proximity and they also enable exploration because they provide a safe base.
3 *The attachment behavioural system*. This is the cognitive component, the mental model the individual has of his/her interrelationship with others.

Attachment theory, as distinct from the earlier maternal deprivation hypothesis, focused on the interpersonal processes which create attachments, most particularly the innate tendency in the infant to seek attachment and to elicit caregiver responses through social releasers.

Evaluation of Bowlby's theory

Rutter's commentary: maternal deprivation reassessed

Michael Rutter published two versions of the book *Maternal deprivation reassessed* (1972, 1981) and offered some key comments and modifications of Bowlby's theory. There were two main conclusions in 1972:

1 Bowlby's hypothesis that 'early life experiences may have serious effects on intellectual and psychosocial development, was no longer controversial'.
2 However the term 'maternal deprivation' covers a 'most heterogeneous range of experiences ... due to quite disparate mechanisms', most notably:

- Antisocial disorders were due to discord at home not separation.
- Affectionless psychopathy was due to the lack (privation) not the loss (deprivation or separation) of love.
- Intellectual delay stems from a lack of cognitive stimulation rather than emotional deprivation.

Rutter's general support for Bowlby should not be overlooked. His aim was not to discredit Bowlby's theory but to make important distinctions in the effects of deprivation.

In 1981, Rutter further noted, after an extensive review of research, that the consequences of deprivation were not as extreme, nor as consistent, nor as irreversible as Bowlby had suggested. Infants and children who do suffer disruption of attachment relations may *also* suffer a variety of *other* problems of early social experience.

Other criticisms of Bowlby's theory

Feminists have objected to Bowlby's doctrine because it appears to suggest that a mother's place is at home with her children (or that one primary caregiver had to remain at home). For many women this has led to guilt and indecision about whether to stay at home or pursue a career. On the other hand, Bowlby's theory also established the central importance of the mother's role. She could now be seen as not simply a provider of food, but an expert in child development.

Bowlby has also been seen as being anti-institutions. He said that bad homes were better than good institutions. To some extent this has been disproved (see Tizard's work where children returned to 'bad homes' did worst of all) but this overlooks the basic issue which was about quality of care. Bowlby was assuming that even a bad home would provide higher quality attachments. His message was to improve the quality of attachments everywhere.

A third issue is Bowlby's argument that the early monotropic relationship forms a template for future relationships. However, this would lead us to expect children to form similar relationships with others but the correlations among a child's various relationships are actually quite low. A child who is securely attached to one caregiver is not necessarily securely attached to others (Main and Weston, 1981).

There has been evidence which links attachment style to later relationships (see p. 48) but this is not a universal finding, for example parent–child relationships are not always positively correlated with child–peer relationships (Howes *et al.*, 1994).

If there are positive correlations, there is an alternative explanation to that of the internal working model. Namely that some infants are simply better than others at forming relationships. Children are born with innate temperamental differences (see p. 21). Children who are appealing to their parents are likely to be appealing to other people, so that a child who does well in one relationship is likely to do well in others (Jacobson and Wille, 1986). Hinde and Stevenson-Hinde suggested that the most reasonable explanation of why these inter-relationship correlations are so low is that behaviours, emotions and cognitions acquired in one relationship are specific to that relationship.

One final point we should note regards the evolutionary argument, which is a *post-hoc* (after the fact) assumption rather than proven fact. In other words, we are making the judgement looking backwards and arguing that a behaviour must be adaptive because it persists. We cannot *know* this is true but are assuming it is likely. It could be that the value of the behaviour is simply neutral rather than positive.

Final analysis

One mark of a good theory is its ability to generate scientific research, which has certainly been true of Bowlby's theory.

His theory is 'correct' insofar as there is good support for the innateness of some attachment behaviours. His theory is doubtful because of the over-estimation of the long-term effects.

The theory fails to account for individual differences and why some children are better able to cope with poor early experiences than others.

Progress exercise

For each of the following state whether you feel the concept is a strength or weakness of Bowlby's theory, and try to explain why.

- Innateness of attachment
- Irreversible effects of early experience
- Monotropy
- Internal working model

Summary

Early theories (Freudian and behaviourist) placed too much value on the relationship between feeding and attachment. Such explanations are flawed in other ways, such as being reductionist and/or based on abnormal behaviour. Bowlby's theory drew on psychoanalytic and ethological models to suggest that attachment was an innately driven process which occurs best during a sensitive period. Maternal deprivation will result in short- and long-term difficulties especially in terms of emotional development. The relationship with a hierarchy of caregivers provides the child with an internal working model for future relationships. The sensitivity and responsiveness of the caregiver is important in establishing the caregiver as a safe base.

Rutter offered a number of points of evaluation, including the fact that Bowlby had muddled lack and loss of attachment. Rutter also felt that more account should be taken of the constellation of factors which may amplify attachment problems. We should also take note of the implications of Bowlby's theory for women's roles and for institutions. Finally, we should consider the idea that the reason some individuals are better able to form relationships throughout life is because they are born that way, rather than because they acquire an adaptive internal working model through secure early attachments.

At the start of the chapter I suggested that a theory of attachment should account for several things, such as the characteristics of attachment figures and the functions of attachment. List what you think are:

1 The desirable characteristics of attachment figures.
2 The main functions of attachment.
3 What other aspects of the attachment process do you think are important?

Review exercise

Further reading

Holmes, J. (1993) *John Bowlby and attachment theory*. London: Routledge. A psychodynamic account of Bowlby's life and his work.

9

Enrichment

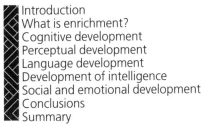
Introduction

This last chapter is a counterpoint to the rest of the book. Thus far, we have identified many of the *negative* effects of privation and deprivation. A more positive approach is to look at ways of enriching children's experiences and environments.

In this chapter we will separately consider various aspects of development: cognitive, social and emotional. However you should remember that these are not easy to separate since, for example, early attachment is intimately related to cognitive development.

What is enrichment?

Much of the research presented here equates enrichment with giving children certain experiences at an earlier age than they might experience them normally. The argument is that, by having these experiences earlier the child is enabled to progress faster and therefore ultimately further than he or she would do otherwise.

A second kind of enrichment is where children are given experiences which they would otherwise lack. Without this, such a lack would result in restricted development. By enriching the child's experience, the potential negative outcomes are avoided.

So we have two kinds of enrichment: programmes to enhance development, and programmes to compensate for deprivation.

Cognitive development

There are many areas of cognitive development to consider, such as perception, language and intelligence. Most research has focused on the latter area.

Perceptual development

The effect of institutionalisation

One of the reasons that children in institutions may suffer intellectual impairment is due to their restricted early *perceptual* experiences. It was the practice in this country, and still is in some Romanian orphanages, to keep institutionalised infants in their cots all day. In such situations infants are inevitably deprived of sensory stimulation. The first stages of cognitive development require such stimulation because perceptual development is the beginning of cognitive development. Infants learn to coordinate what they 'sense' (see, hear, etc.) with their motor control. For example, they see an object waving in front of their eyes and come to realise it is their own hand. Piaget not surprisingly called the first stage of cognitive development the **sensorimotor stage**.

The importance of perception for cognitive development would lead us to expect differences, in terms of cognitive development, between children reared in visually deprived environments and those reared in normal environments. White and Held (1966) tested this by enriching the visual environments of some very young institution-alised infants. When they were less than a month old the infants were given red and white mitts and multicoloured sheets. After a few months this 'enriched' group was compared with a control group using 'hand regard' as the measure of perceptual and cognitive devel-opment (infants who spent longer looking at their hands were judged to be more perceptually, and therefore cognitively, advanced – though this is debatable). White and Held found that the enriched infants did engage in hand regard at a much earlier age than the control group. We have no evidence of the long-term consequences of this interven-tion but it does show that perceptual enrichment can speed up development and suggests that there may be serious consequences of visual deprivation.

Other studies of visual deprivation

In general, evidence about the effects of visual deprivation comes mainly from non-human studies because of the greater ethical diffi-culties in depriving humans of early visual experiences. Such animal studies have found that the visual system depends on stimulation in order to develop and, if visual experiences are absent or limited during a critical period, the visual system will be permanently damaged. For example, Blakemore and Cooper (1970) raised kittens in a drum with only vertical black and white stripes and found that, later, the kittens were unable to respond to horizontal lines. They reacted to table legs (vertical lines) but tripped over ropes stretched in front of them (horizontal lines).

There is some human evidence to corroborate these permanent effects of restricted early experience on the visual system. Banks *et al.* (1975) studied children born with squint eyesight, a condition where the two eyes do not coordinate properly. The effect of this is that the input from the eyes (binocular vision) doesn't match, which limits visual precision. The defect can be corrected with an operation. However Banks *et al.* found that if this wasn't done before the age of 4, such children suffered permanently impaired binocular vision. In other words, after a critical age their visual system was no longer capable of change.

Conclusion

Therefore, there are two potential effects of early sensory deprivation: (1) cognitive delays which affect general cognitive development and (2) permanent damage to the parts of the brain which interpret sensory data. Das (1973) suggested that one of the reasons for cognitive disabilities is sensory deprivation and that, by enriching a child's home and educational environment, such disabilities can be overcome.

Language development

Linguistic enrichment

Bernstein (1961) introduced the concept of two different forms of language: an **elaborated** and **restricted code**. The former kind of language allows a user to articulate abstract concepts more easily and, Bernstein suggested, is more likely to be used by middle-class parents and their children whereas lower-class families are more likely to use a restricted code. According to Bernstein's **verbal deprivation theory** (a term used by Labov, 1969), this language difference may explain why lower-class children may have limited cognitive development – restricted linguistic code limits cognitive development.

If this is true then it follows that enriched language experience should increase cognitive development in lower-class children. To test this Schwartz *et al.* (1967) studied two groups of socially disadvantaged primary school children over a period of two years. One group received enriched schooling, including work involving their use of language. The researchers found significant differences on a test of psycholinguistic abilities, supporting the hypothesis that early enrichment helps to offset language disability caused by social disadvantage.

Further support comes from a study by Fowler (1990) which assessed a linguistic enrichment programme designed for parents to use with their very young children. The programme involved language-related games and play. Fowler found that there were significant gains, for example the children used pronouns such as 'him', at 18 months which was 5 months earlier than usual. Of course the question remains about how long these gains might last.

In contrast, a study by Sinclair-de-Zwart (1969) suggested that linguistic enrichment may not affect cognitive development. This study was conducted to test an aspect of Piaget's theory of cognitive development, namely that cognitive development precedes and underlies linguistic development, not vice versa. Sinclair-de-Zwart noted first of all that children who couldn't cope with conservation tasks were also behind in their linguistic development. ('Conservation' is the ability to comprehend that volume or mass stays the same even when a thing looks physically different, as when you pour water from a thin beaker into a wide one.) The study by Sinclair-de-Zwart also found that, even if one tried to teach non-conserving children to use words such as 'bigger' or 'more' (linguistic enrichment), the children's ability to conserve was not improved. This suggests that linguistic enrichment may not always enhance cognitive development.

Criticisms of verbal deprivation theory

There were critics of Bernstein's view, most notably Labov (1970) who suggested that Bernstein failed to understand the subtleties of non-standard English and therefore his view that lower-class language was restricted was mistaken. In fact, Labov argued, non-standard English is equally capable of representing abstract thought and Bernstein may have simply confused linguistic and social deprivation.

A further line of argument can be presented in terms of the debate between language and thought – the debate that either the language one uses affects one's thinking and cognitive development, or thought exists independently of language. We haven't room here to present both sides of the cause but Flanagan (1996) argued that there is no convincing evidence that language is a prerequisite for thought.

One further point, in relation to the concept of linguistic enrichment programmes, is that such programmes tend to run into political difficulties because the language of any sub-culture is intimately bound up with its social identity and therefore people are very resistant to being taught alternative dialects.

Reading

Learning to read is related to language development. One of the key questions is whether it is '**readiness**' (maturity) which determines when children start to read or whether enrichment can improve reading, and thus cognitive development.

115

Empirical evidence for the importance of maturity comes from a study by Gibson *et al.* (1962). They showed letter-like figures to children and asked them to identify the same shape in various transformations, such as at 90° to the original figure. Children under the age of 5 had difficulty with this task, which suggests that their ability to discriminate visual stimuli was not sufficiently mature to cope with reading.

On the other hand, practice may overcome such apparent immaturity. Bryant and Bradley (1983) worked with a group of primary school children who had difficulty discriminating sounds. They taught the children sound categorisation skills and found significant improvements in reading.

Speech

Many children suffer speech difficulties, such as stuttering or poor pronunciation. They may be given early remedial help in the form of enrichment programmes to ensure that their social and cognitive development is not affected.

Development of intelligence

Hothousing

There are some people who believe that if children receive extra stimulation during early development they will experience significant and lasting IQ gains. The term 'hothousing' was coined to suggest that the same process could be used with children as is used with vegetables to force them to ripen early.

Logan (1987) claimed that he was able to produce children with IQs of an astonishing 160 using a programme of **prenatal** stimulation (the average IQ is 100). Such programmes involve talking to children while they are in their mother's wombs. They have had very little if any empirical support. The size of the benefits alone are enough to lead one to suspect the validity of Logan's claims.

Howe (1998) claimed that hothousing during childhood, as distinct from prenatal enrichment, is possible but requires a great deal of intensive training and high levels of motivation. Kunkel (1985) has provided an example of this in his description of seventeenth-century orphan girls in Venice. The girls became renowned for their musical talents and people flocked from all over Europe to hear them. There was nothing innately talented about the girls; we can deduce this because they came from many different families. However they shared an important and enriching experience in being given intensive musical training during childhood. But perhaps even more importantly, they had the motivation to excel because those who exhibited talent were more marriageable and therefore would escape from the institution to a better life. This supports the view that it is motivation even more than experience which accelerates development.

Indeed, Feldman (1986) concluded from studies of many child prodigies that the distinguishing characteristic of such children is their burning passion to succeed. It is likely that parents who place their children in hothouse programmes will be highly motivated themselves and this is likely to affect their children. Therefore we can probably better explain the success of hothouse programmes in terms of motivation rather than enrichment.

Preschool enrichment programmes

Perhaps the best known and most extensive preschool enrichment programme is Operation Headstart. In the 1960s there was a political move in the United States to set up an intervention programme which would help disadvantaged children. It was argued that such children lacked some of the early benefits enjoyed by more middle-class children with regard to, for example, health and intellectual stimulation, and that therefore they were disadvantaged even before they started school. Such disadvantages inevitably only got worse and perpetuated a cycle of failure.

In 1965 the first Headstart programmes were run involving half a million children. When the children were compared with a control group after the first year there were small IQ gains, however these were short-lived and the financial costs of the programme were over one million dollars (Zigler and Muenchow, 1992). Follow-up studies presented a more encouraging picture. Lazar and Darlington (1982) reported that the Headstart children were less likely to be placed in special classes, were more likely to go to college and, in te~ social benefits, were less likely to need welfare assistanc~

delinquent. Seitz (1990) also found higher IQs in the Headstart children when they were tested in adolescence, suggesting a delayed effect.

One note of caution, in terms of methodology, is that the control groups may not have actually been comparable because allocation to such groups was not strictly random.

Another explanation for the weak benefits of the Headstart programme is that the children involved may already have been too old at the time they were first given enrichment, and that in addition greater parental involvement may have been desirable. Subsequent programmes have attempted to address these possibilities. For example, the Carolina Abecedarian Project (Ramey, 1993) focused on low intelligence mothers and their infants, running a special daycare programme from infancy and giving extra medical attention. By school age the children had higher IQs than a control group but this declined soon thereafter.

More impressive results were found by the Milwaukee project (Heber *et al.*, 1972), a programme designed to offer massive environmental enrichment to improve the IQs of infants born to retarded lower-class Black mothers (IQs under 75). Half the group were controls and received no extra treatment, the other mothers were given help with job-related skills, parenting and housekeeping. The infants were placed in a regular daycare programme from the age of 3 months which taught the infants preschool skills and also involved the mothers.

By the time the children started school they had a mean IQ of 124 compared with 94 for the control group. Gilhousen *et al.* (1990) found that this gap had decreased from 30 to 10 IQ points by the time the participants were 12 years old, however the difference was still significant. There were again methodological flaws similar to those in the Headstart programme and Gilhousen *et al.* concluded that the study provided only minimal support for the benefits of early intervention.

Other programmes have been shorter term and involved slightly older children. For example, Portnoy *et al.* (1973) ran a summer day camp for 6–8-year-old inner city children which focused on educational and cognitive enrichment, as well as social awareness and growth. It was reported that the campers showed significant gains in abstract conceptual thinking and self-image.

In many of the enrichment programmes attention was giv child's health as well as cognitive stimulation. Enriching a cl may well have major consequences. Benton and Cook (199., .ouilu significant IQ increments in children who were given vitamin supplements. Two groups of children were compared. Both groups thought they were receiving supplements but in fact half of the children received placebo (fake) supplements. The reason for using placebos was to rule out the effects of expectations – if the children thought they were going to improve, this alone might have increased their test performance.

Further support for the value of nutritional enrichment comes from Lynn (1986) who suggested that the reason why average IQ scores continue to rise must be due to improved nutrition rather than, for example, genetic change. In Japan the average rise per decade is 7.7 points whereas it is 1.7 points in the UK, which must be due to greater annual improvements in diet in Japan whereas diet has been good in the UK for some time and therefore improvement is now slower.

Intelligence enrichment programmes: conclusions

It would seem that there may often be short term benefits from enrichment programmes, but not long term benefits. This is likely to be because there are so many other factors which affect the development of intelligence. Or it may be that intelligence is largely inherited and therefore fixed. Many psychologists support this latter view and Herrnstein and Murray (1994) argued that, if intelligence is inherited, it means that it would be better to spend money on educating people in a manner appropriate to their intelligence level rather than trying to increase it using enrichment programmes. In contrast, Howe (1998) maintained that there is substantial evidence that intelligence is not fixed, for example how else could we explain the short term gains achieved in the enrichment studies described above?

The question of how money is best spent is difficult to calculate because there are so many different ways to measure the costs versus the benefits. Davenport (1991) reported that for every $1,000 spent on the Headstart programme, $4,000 were saved in terms of welfare benefits and policing. In contrast Haskins (1989) claimed that the reverse was true!

Progress exercise

1 Name one example of a compensatory enrichment programme and one of a programme which enhanced normal development.
2 For each suggest one methodological or ethical factor which is important in evaluating the findings.

Social and emotional development

Popularity

Some children are more popular than others, and this popularity appears to be a feature of the individual rather than the social group because the same children are popular even when placed in different groups. 'Rejected' children may lack important social skills and have a self-expectation of failure on the basis of past experience (Shaffer, 1993). Enrichment programmes which give such children an opportunity to learn and practise interpersonal social skills have been reasonably successful. For example, Oden and Asher (1977) worked with 8- and 9-year-old social isolates and taught them how to take turns, communicate effectively, and help peers. They found that the children became more outgoing and positive, and a year later had increased their social status within their peer groups.

Furman *et al.* (1979) used younger-peer therapy to help withdrawn preschool children. The children were given special play sessions with children who were either the same age as the withdrawn children or 18 months younger. At the end of the course both sets of children had became more socially outgoing than a control group, but the ones helped by younger children did best of all. The reason for this may be because withdrawn children are developmentally backwards and therefore younger playmates can offer a more appropriate level of interaction. Harlow used a similar method of 'peer therapy' with his monkeys (see p. 33).

Attachment

One way to enrich children's attachment experiences is through improving the quality of day care for those children whose mothers work. Quality and frequency of adult–child interactions are critical variables, and adults who respond sensitively to infant signals affect the development of the child's social and cognitive abilities. There are programmes designed to improve these qualities in day-care workers (see Howes p. 80).

Enrichment is also possible by working with parents. Brody (1978) assessed a treatment and enrichment programme called 'Developmental Play'. The aim of the programme was to stimulate or rebuild the bonding relationship between a parent and an emotionally disturbed child. Programme leaders worked with about seven pairs of parents and their children, encouraging them to interact more effectively. The results were promising.

Conclusions

Any positive intervention technique used in relation to a child's development could be considered as enrichment. For example, in the 1930s a study by McGraw (cited in Howe, 1995) showed that children's physical abilities (running, jumping and climbing) could be significantly accelerated if they were given regular daily practice. Television programmes such as *Sesame Street*, and access to books are all forms of enrichment.

At the beginning of this chapter I distinguished between programmes of enrichment which lead to *accelerated* development as distinct from interventions which *compensate* for actual lack of experience or deprivation. The former may well have rather short-lasting effects. The latter may significantly alter a person's life, and may have to take place before a certain age, as was the case for perceptual development.

One final point I would like to make concerns the ethics of this research. Enrichment programmes clearly intend to offer positive benefits for the participants and therefore we would not object to such research. However, since control groups are necessary for any conclusive research, this means that some children were denied access to these benefits and this may be ethically questionable. Equally, it might

121

be the case that enriching experience may change group dynamics and formerly 'normal' children may end up relatively impoverished.

Summary

Enrichment may be either in terms of accelerated learning or compensation for potential deprivation. Enrichment programmes can enhance perceptual, linguistic, intellectual, social and/or emotional development through, for example, increases in stimulation, motivation, nutrition and interpersonal interactions. It is possible that some of the effects of such programmes are permanent, for example for speech and emotional development. On the other hand, some accelerated development and compensatory programmes may have only short-term effects, such as some hothousing programmes and projects like Headstart.

Review exercise

Describe and evaluate two (or more) enrichment studies that support the view that early experience does matter, and two that suggest the contrasting view.

Further reading

Howe, M.J.A. (1990) *Sense and nonsense about hothouse children: a practical guide for parents and teachers*. Leicester: BPS books. A thorough examination of the question of whether geniuses are born or made, written for the general reader as well as the psychology student.

Zigler, E. and Muenchow, S. (1992) *Head Start: the insider story of America's most successful educational experiment*. New York: Basic Books. All the details of the Headstart programme.

10

Study aids

IMPROVING YOUR ESSAY WRITING SKILLS

At this point in the book you have acquired the knowledge necessary
to tackle the exam itself. Answering exam questions is a skill and in
this chapter we hope to help you improve this skill. A common
mistake that some students make is not providing the kind of
evidence the examiner is looking for. Another is failing to properly
answer the question, despite providing lots of information. Typically,
a grade C answer is accurate and reasonably constructed, but has
limited detail and commentary. To lift such an answer to an A or B
grade may require no more than fuller detail, better use of material
and a coherent organisation. By studying the essays below, and the
comments that follow, you can learn how to turn your grade C answer
into a grade A. Please note that marks given by the examiner in the
practice essays should be used as a guide only and are not definitive.
They represent the 'raw marks' given by an AEB examiner. That is, the
marks the examiner would give to the examining board based on a
total of 24 marks per question broken down into Skill A (description)
and Skill B (evaluation). A table showing this scheme is in Appendix
C of Paul Humphreys' series title, *Exam Success in AEB Psychology*.
They may not be the marks given on the examination certificate
received ultimately by the student because all examining boards are

required to use a common standardised system called the Uniform Mark Scale (UMS) which adjusts all raw scores to a single standard acceptable to all examining boards.

The essays are about the length a student would be able to write in 35–40 minutes (leaving extra time for planning and checking). Each essay is followed by detailed comments about its strengths and weaknesses. The most common problems to look for are:

- Students frequently fail to answer the actual question set, and present 'one they made earlier' (the *Blue Peter* answer).
- Many weak essays suffer from a lack of evaluation or commentary.
- On the other hand, sometimes students go too far in the other direction and their essays are all evaluation. Description is vital in demonstrating your knowledge and understanding of the selected topic.
- Don't write 'everything you know' in the hope that something will get credit. Excellence is displayed through selectivity and therefore improvements can often be made by *removing* material which is irrelevant to the question set.

For more ideas about how to write good essays you should consult *Exam Success in AEB Psychology* (in this series) by Paul Humphreys.

Practice essay 1

'It has been a continuing source of controversy in psychology as to whether early experiences have important effects on an individual's subsequent social development.'

Critically consider ways in which studies of deprivation and/or enrichment in childhood help us to resolve this controversy. **(24 marks)**

AEB January 1998

Starting point: One of the problems with this question is that there is so much that you could include that you run the risk of writing too much in terms of breadth and sacrificing details (depth). The injunction 'critically consider' requires you to present your knowledge and understanding of studies related to deprivation and/or enrichment, and to discuss the strengths and weaknesses of this material.

Note that the question does not ask you specifically to address the quotation in your answer, but it does ask you to consider specific 'studies' rather than research (which is both theory and/or studies) in general. Therefore the 'meat' of your answer will be the empirical studies with which you are familiar. These should be described carefully. Each should be considered in terms of what is demonstrated (strength) and methodological flaws (weaknesses). Theories can be used to assess the value or implications of any study.

Candidate's answer

A lot of research has been conducted in trying to discover what effects early deprivation has on development. Research has also looked at the effects of enrichment, which is a more positive approach.

Koluchová studied twins who spent much of their early lives locked in a cupboard. They had little human contact other than between themselves and no other stimulation. The children were discovered when they were 7 years old and taken into care. As they have got older it was found that they recovered reasonably well and have been able to form attachments.

This suggests that early deprivation can be recovered from, though the twins did have each other which may have meant that they did have early attachments. It is also difficult to generalise from such a small sample.

The evidence from the Koluchová study appears to disprove Bowlby's theory about the importance of early attachments. Bowlby did research into 44 juvenile thieves and compared them to other children who had psychiatric problems. He found that the difference between the two groups was that the thieves had almost all experienced early separations from their parents. Bowlby suggested that these separations at an early age harmed their emotional development and they developed affectionless psychopathy. This meant they were more likely to become thieves rather than just being maladjusted like the control group.

Rutter criticised Bowlby's research saying that Bowlby didn't distinguish between privation and deprivation. Privation is when someone has not formed an attachment whereas to be deprived means that you had the attachment but it was taken away. The thieves in

Bowlby's study may have been separated but they didn't necessarily lack affection.

Hodges and Tizard studied children in a children's home. All of them had no attachments before the age of 2 and many of them were only adopted at the age of 4. The children who were adopted recovered reasonably well. This shows that children can cope with having no love early in life.

Another study which looked at institutions found that the children recovered well if they were placed in a ward for backward women. Skodak and Skeels showed that children who were placed in such wards had large IQ increases which was presumably because they got more attention. This kind of study offers a more positive approach to the study of deprivation. Some psychologists have criticised this research because the children may have responded to the researchers expectations and this is why they improved.

A lot of research has also looked at the effects of enrichment. Operation Headstart was a programme set up to give special help to disadvantaged preschool children so they could cope better when they started school. The children had help with skills for reading and writing, as well as special medical attention. At first they did well at school but when they were tested later the differences were rather small compared to a control group. This was disappointing.

Examiner's comment

The candidate has focused on studies, as required in the question. The range is somewhat limited and, though some details have been included, there could have been a lot more description and elaboration.

The candidate has tried to present commentary and interpretation, for example 'enrichment, which is a more positive approach' or 'This meant they were more likely to become thieves rather than just being maladjusted like the control group.' It is vital to use all the material as effectively as possible and this means explaining the relevance of any material.

Evaluation has also been achieved through the use of theoretical arguments, namely those of Bowlby and Rutter, and through methodological criticisms. All of this material would have benefited from greater elaboration.

The essay is reasonably structured but there is a kind of 'stream of consciousness effect' in that it feels as if the candidate is reeling off whatever comes to mind rather than working to a plan. On the other hand, all the material is relevant which shows a focus and a degree of selectivity.

The candidate has shown *some* knowledge and understanding, and an ability to be critical about the material described. However, overall it is a *limited* response.

Clearly the essay would be improved by a greater range of empirical evidence and evaluation, taking care not to repeat the same evaluations each time. One might for example, look at the ethics of conducting deprivation or even enrichment studies. The essay would have also benefited from the inclusion of greater detail to demonstrate familiarity with the studies.

This essay would receive 6 (description) + 6 (evaluation) = 12/24, which is equivalent to a weak Grade C.

Practice essay 2

Discuss the view that cultural differences in childrearing practices are an important factor in the socialisation of the child.
(24 marks)
AEB Summer 1997

Starting point: 'Discuss' requires the candidate to both describe and evaluate. Here that means you need to describe certain childrearing practices in the context of socialisation, and then assess to what extent the practices have or have not influenced the child's social development. The problem here is relating what you know about cross-cultural research to the issue of socialisation, and avoiding just writing what you know about attachment, or other aspects of child-rearing.

Socialisation is the process by which children take on their culture. This is specifically things like learning morals, gender identity and language - topics you may be familiar with from other areas of the syllabus. Socialisation can broadly be interpreted to mean anything the child learns in a cultural context.

127

In this essay you can use empirical evidence as part of your description of cultural differences, or you could use empirical evidence to evaluate the strength and/or weakness of any theoretical argument.

Candidate's answer

Some psychologists believe that childrearing practices are entirely responsible for the social development of the child whereas others believe there are important innate factors which account for socialisation. Which is it, nature or nurture?

In order to answer this question psychologists use cross-cultural studies because there are different childrearing practices in different cultures and this means we can see if the different methods have different outcomes.

Our culture, today, aims to raise children in a loving environment and to provide stable, secure attachments for the children. These attachments give the child a secure base for exploring the world about them. This means they develop into independent and curious individuals. We can relate this to the ideals of our society which is for people to develop personally and intellectually. We live in an individualistic society.

Other societies have been described as collectivistic. Nobles argued that the African self concept involved 'we' rather than 'I'. This kind of culture may provide children with multiple attachments because their future interactions within the society will be less singular.

However, studies of cultures where children are cared for by lots of people still show that attachments are often formed with one main figure. For example, the Efe, a pygmy tribe studied by Tronick *et al.* (1992) live in extended family groups. Even though the infants are looked after by whatever person is nearest and they are even breastfed by other women, they still formed the closest bond with their mother. This may be because they slept with their mothers and therefore spent most time, in the end, with her. On the other hand, it may be that the researchers were biased and their observations were mistaken. Cross-cultural research is very difficult to conduct because the observers are inevitably biased by their own cultural expectations. They may see what they want to see or they see things in terms of how they have learned to interpret the world.

Other cross-cultural studies have found that infants can be treated very differently, yet grow up to be quite similar to Western children. Kagan and Klein (1973) studied a small Guatemalan community. The villagers believed that dust and dirt was very bad for their children and therefore they virtually locked their infants up for the first year, allowing them very little contact with anyone and giving them no toys. They were even kept in darkness. At the end of their first year the children were allowed outside and began to interact normally, that is like Western children do. When the Guatemalan children were first assessed they were quite backwards for their age but when they were tested later, around the age of 10, they performed at levels equivalent to Western children. This suggests that early deprivation does not irreversibly affect development.

A study by Munroe and Munroe (1980) related cultural practices to a culture's general view of life. Munroe and Munroe spent a long time observing the Logoli of Western Kenya. The children were very much indulged during infancy, being held a lot by their mothers and other caregivers, and also quite protected. Munroe and Munroe felt that this was the culture's way of promoting their rather gentle and indulgent way of life.

In contrast, a different culture, the Mundugumour who were studied by Mead (1935), brought their children up in a very loveless and harsh manner. As a tribe the Mundugumour were very aggressive and warlike and therefore it is not surprising that they used such methods.

We can also look at culture differences within our own culture. Maccoby (1980) found that lower class parents stress obedience more than higher class parents, who stress curiosity and independence. It may be that classes and cultures which are poorer cannot afford independence and curiosity.

All these studies show that different cultures use different methods and these are related to the way adults in that society behave. But this is correlational evidence. We don't know that the childrearing method has *caused* the behaviour. It could be that there are personality differences which are innate in each culture and the methods which are used are the best ones for the personality type.

129

Examiner's comment

The candidate started the essay off with a question, about nature and nurture, but then never really got round to answering it. Such a lack of direction is not desirable but in exam conditions one cannot expect too much, and the ethos of positive marking means there would be no penalties.

The rest of the essay did manage to flow quite nicely and demonstrate a reasonable level of knowledge and understanding. The range of research (theory and/or studies) is perhaps slightly limited but this is balanced by quite a good amount of detail. Using researchers' names and dates gives a sense of competence to the essay.

The student offered some interpretation and evaluation of the material described, and the last paragraph was especially useful in offering a general criticism of the evidence.

As always the essay would have benefited by greater breadth though not at a cost of the kind of detail included here. Some of the points made could have been given a more thorough discussion, for example the student might have explained more clearly the childrearing methods we use in our society to raise individualistic children.

This essay would receive 8 (description) + 6 (evaluation) = 14/24, which is equivalent to a weak Grade B.

Practice essay 3

Describe and evaluate psychological research into the development of sociability *and/or* attachments in early childhood.
(24 marks)
AEB Summer 1998

Starting point: It might be tempting to write a rather similar answer to this question as for the first one. Clearly some of the same evidence would be relevant. Indeed many students have a prepared 'attachment essay'. The danger of using this approach is that you are likely to lose marks because you will inevitably not be answering the question set. It is relatively easy for an examiner to spot such prepared answers.

In this question you are asked to focus on the development of attachments rather than the effects of deprivation. You could also widen the scope of the essay to include sociability as well as attachment but should be wary of trying to include too much material at a sacrifice of detail/depth.

Note that the term 'research' refers to either theory or empirical evidence, or both.

Candidate's answer

I will write about how infants form attachments in early childhood.

When a baby is born they have a variety of behaviours which make adults take an interest in them. They smile and cry, and interact with any adults. These are inborn behaviours which make adults become attached to the infants. They are especially important because they keep adults close to the infant, to provide protection and food. If an infant is left on their own they start to cry and then someone should come running.

As well as infant behaviour which is innately programmed to encourage caregiving, adults also respond innately to babies. They feel uncomfortable when they hear a baby cry and they smile when a baby coos. Not all cultures respond this way so it may not be inborn.

When babies get to the age of about 7 months they form their first specific attachments. Until this time they are happy with any adult but by the age of 7 months they cry if one particular adult leaves the room and they are most comforted by this one adult.

Why do babies become attached to this one person? Freud suggested it was because the mother gives the baby food and oral gratification. The baby comes to love the person who feeds them. The behaviourists thought it was more or less for the same reason. The baby associates the person who feeds them with pleasure and the caregiver becomes a conditioned reinforcer.

Harlow did some research with monkeys which showed that this wasn't the reason for attachment. There was a bare wire 'mother' and a cloth covered one. The feeding bottle was attached to the bare wire mother. The monkeys spent most of their time with the cloth mother and especially ran to 'her' when they were frightened. This suggested that it was not feeding that created attachment but comfort.

Bowlby extended this theory and suggested that infants and young children should not be separated from their caregivers because that breaks the attachment bonds and leads to affectionless psychopathy.

Harlow did find that the monkeys who had these fake mothers grew up to be quite maladjusted. And Bowlby found the same in his study of 44 thieves.

Another thing which is important for the development of attachments is the sensitivity of the caregiver. Ainsworth developed the idea that infants become most strongly attached to someone who is most responsive to them.

Infants have more than one attachment. Soon after they form one main attachment they form other attachments as well. Different people give them different things. For example Lamb said that fathers are good for rough and tumble play.

Examiner's comment

The student used both theory and empirical research to answer this question. The answer is reasonably structured, providing a useful answer to this question. All the way through, however, the student could have provided more detail for the material described. For example, the 44 thieves study is only mentioned in passing and Ainsworth's research is given very superficial treatment. Alternatively the student could have provided greater breadth and looked at other explanations for why attachments form, such as the factors underlying the difference between secure and insecure attachments.

The student has used a good strategy in occasionally starting a paragraph with the essay title, which serves to remind both the writer and the reader of the question which is being answered. The essay was well focused on the question but there was simply a limited amount of detail and material. The breadth could have been increased by looking, for example, at the research related to very early physical contact and bonding, the stability of attachments through childhood, and the short-term effects of attachments.

The evaluation is very basic indeed. This could have been improved by elaborating the material on culture and Bowlby's empirical research. In addition some further commentary could have been added such as giving some of the criticisms of Bowlby's theory and/or evidence to support Ainsworth's hypothesis. The essay ends very abruptly, it would have been helpful to write some sort of conclusion which could be credited as evaluation.

This essay would receive 6 (description) + 4 (evaluation) = 10/24, which is equivalent to a weak Grade D.

KEY RESEARCH SUMMARIES

Article 1

Bowlby, J. (1946) *Forty-four juvenile thieves*. **London: Balliére, Tindall and Cox.**

Introduction

This study counts as a classic in the area of attachment research and is a favourite with students, who often describe it in their essays and use it to support Bowlby's maternal deprivation hypothesis. This summary is an attempt to ensure that you can argue on the basis of clear information rather than a mere glimpse of the details.

Background

John Bowlby worked as a psychiatrist in a Child Guidance Clinic in London just before the Second World War. Around the same time several other psychologists conducted and reported research which indicated that separations from caregivers could have serious and long-term effects. For example, Spitz and Wolf (1946) studied children in hospital and found that they progressively became more withdrawn and apathetic. If the separations continued for over three months this turned into severe depression (anaclitic depression), with a poor prognosis of recovery.

Bowlby's theory was that early separations disrupt the bonding process between caregiver and child and this leads to long-term depression and psychopathy.

Research question: Can maladjustment in later life be explained in terms of early emotional traumas, particularly early separation between mother and child?

METHOD   There were two distinctive features noted about all the children studied:

1   Some displayed an 'affectionless' character. This is a lack of normal affection, shame or sense of responsibility.
2   Some of the children had suffered 'early and prolonged separations from their mothers'. In practice this meant that, at least before the age of 2, these children had continually or repeatedly been in foster homes or hospitals, often not visited by their families. Children who were adopted early and therefore had a stable maternal relationship in early life were not included in the study.

RESULTS

Table 10.1 **Differences between the delinquents and the control group**

Type of case	Separated from mother	Not separated	Total
Affectionless thieves	12	2	14
Other thieves	5	25	30
All thieves	17	27	44
Control participants	2	42	44

DISCUSSION

However, the evidence was *flawed* in several respects:

1   The data about separation was collected retrospectively. Parents of the children attending the clinic were asked to describe their child's earlier experiences. Inevitably such recall is not entirely accurate.
2   The data were correlational which means that we cannot be sure that maternal separation *caused* the affectionless character. In fact the children were not just separated from their mothers but experienced traumatic disruptions of their early years, for example some of them were separated because they spent time in hospital. Rutter (1972) suggested that families where children experienced separations also tended to have other problems such as poor living conditions and marital discord. These factors could explain the ultimate outcome as well as maternal separations.

3   The diagnosis 'affectionless' may not have been reliable. It was made on the basis of reports from relatives and interviews with the psychiatrist (Bowlby). Both sources may have been biased.

Nevertheless, the picture that Bowlby painted of some of the children's lives leaves a very strong impression and one of his chief concerns was the unnecessary separation of mother and child, for example, during hospital treatment.

DISCUSSION QUESTIONS

1   Why is this described as a 'retrospective, naturalistic study'?
2   The experimental and control groups differed in terms of their delinquency. What emotional differences were there between the two groups?
3   What conclusion would you reach on the basis of the study's results, taking the potential flaws into account?

Article 2

Schaffer, H. R. and Emerson, P. E. (1964) The development of social attachments in infancy. *Monographs of the Society for Research in Child Development*, **29 (3 Serial No. 94)**

Introduction

This remains the largest longitudinal study of infant attachment behaviour. Schaffer and Emerson collected a wealth of data from their detailed observations of 60 infants from a mainly working-class area of Glasgow. The infants were studied over a period of 2 years.

Background

The dominant view of attachment prior to Bowlby was that of behaviourism. This suggested that attachment was related to reinforcement gained through feeding. Schaffer and Emerson claimed that this had exercised a 'stranglehold' on research which was finally relieved by Harlow's evidence that it was not merely physical contact nor feeding which led to attachment. Bowlby's theory also influenced the movement away from learning theory, proposing instead that social tendencies are innate and these are expressed in behaviours which tie the mother to the child from the beginning.

Schaffer and Emerson felt that, in order to progress this theory further, more data was needed about the parameters of the attachment process.

Research aims: To supply descriptive data about attachment. Specifically to explore the age at onset, the intensity and the objects of attachment, plus to search for any individual differences.

METHOD   Attachment was measured in terms of separation protest in seven everyday situations: the infant was left alone in a room, left with other people, left in his/her pram outside the house, left in his pram outside the shops, left in his cot at night, put down after being held by an adult, or passed by while sitting in his cot or chair.

Information about the infant's responses were gathered by interviewing the child's mother at every visit. Mothers were also asked generally about situations where separation protest was shown, and to whom these protests were directed. This meant that the researchers could rate the intensity of attachment at each monthly visit. They used a 4-point scale where 0 was 'no protest recorded' and 3 'the infant cries loudly on each occasion'.

Schaffer and Emerson also measured stranger anxiety by starting every visit by approaching the infant and noting at what point the infant started to whimper, thus displaying anxiety.

RESULTS

1   Age of onset. Half of the children showed their first specific attachment between 25 and 32 weeks (6–8 months). Four of the children were slightly younger and six of the children were older than 11 months. Fear of strangers occurred about a month later in all the children.

2   Intensity. This peaked in the first month after attachment behaviour first appeared. It was measured by the strength of separation protest. However there were large individual differences. Intensely attached infants had mothers who responded quickly to their demands (high responsiveness) and who offered the child the most interaction. Infants who were weakly attached had mothers who failed to interact.

3   Objects of attachment. Soon after one main attachment was formed, the infants also became attached to other people. By 18 months very few (13 per cent) were attached to only one person, 31 per cent had five or more attachments, such as the father, grandparent or older sibling.

In 65 per cent of the children the first specific attachment was to the mother, and in a further 30 per cent the mother was the first joint object of attachment. Fathers were rarely the first sole object of attachment (3 per cent) but 27 per cent of them were the joint first object.

4   Time spent with infant: In 39 per cent of the cases the person who usually fed, bathed and changed the child was *not* the child's primary attachment object. In other words, many of the mothers were not the person who performed these tasks yet they were the main attachment object.

DISCUSSION QUESTIONS

1   Compare the method of measuring attachment behaviour used here with the Strange Situation. Suggest at least one advantage and one disadvantage of this method.
2   What comments might you make about the ethics of this study? Again you could compare this with the Strange Situation method.
3   What criticisms might you make about the sample used in this study?

Article 3

Fox, N. (1977) Attachment of kibbutz infants to mother and metapelet. *Child Development*, 48, 1,228–1,239.

Introduction

Cross-cultural studies are useful for answering a variety of questions, such as to see whether specific child-rearing techniques have specific outcomes, or to determine whether certain behaviours are universal and therefore quite possibly innate. In the case of Fox's study, a further question was the effects of the kind of child care on the formation of attachments.

Background

In Israel, at the time of this investigation, about 2 per cent of the population lived on kibbutzim. These are agricultural settlements where everything is shared, including childminding. Communal child care begins when the infant is 4 days old. He or she is placed in an infant house and cared for by a trained nurse called a **metapelet**. The mother remains off work for six weeks and spends time with her child but the child sleeps in the infant house. At about 4 months the child is placed in the care of another metapelet. The metapelet is responsible for feeding, clothing and socialising the child. Children of 1½ typically spend about three hours a day with their parents.

This form of caregiving offered the opportunity to conduct a naturalistic experiment in comparing the effects of multiple caretaking on infant emotional development.

Research aims: Does the person who spends most time with an infant become their main attachment figure? Are there differences in terms of quality in the attachments that a child has with his/her mother or metapelet?

METHOD Attachment behaviour was assessed using a variation of the Strange Situation involving thirteen episodes. The additional episodes were designed to include the metapelet as well as the mother, so there were occasions when both were present and when one left or the other left the infant. This way it was possible to compare the child's attachments to both women.

RESULTS The children protested equally when either mother or metapelet left. However there was a difference in the behaviour shown at reunion, favouring the mother. More children sought their mother and were more comforted by her.

DISCUSSION It would appear that children are attached to both caretakers but most children were more securely or strongly attached to their mother. Therefore time spent with the caretaker cannot be the chief factor in attachment behaviour. Instead it may be that mothers offer greater sensitivity and responsiveness to their own child and this creates a stronger attachment.

DISCUSSION   The metapelet spends much of her time in routine child-minding activity rather than focusing attention on the child, whereas the mother does not have to do any of that in the short time she and her child are together.

We should remember, however, that some of the metapelets had only been with the children for four months. In general there was quite a high turnover rate of metapelets and therefore they would have little vested interest in forming long-term relationships with the children, i.e. forming emotional bonds with them.

We should also remember that this is a cross-cultural study. It may be that the Strange Situation was not an appropriate way to measure attachment behaviour in this culture.

DISCUSSION QUESTIONS

1   What does this study tell us about the innateness of attachment behaviours?
2   What does the study tell us about the effects of different childrearing methods?
3   What might we conclude about the effects of day care in our own culture?

Glossary

The first occurrence of each of these terms is highlighted in **bold** type in the main text. An asterisk has been used to indicate that a word or phrase has an entry of its own in this glossary.

adaptiveness The extent to which a behaviour increases the reproduction potential of an individual and therefore the survival of its genes*.

affectionless psychopathy A condition described by Bowlby where individuals appear to experience little guilt or emotion, lack normal affection, and are unable to form permanent and emotionally meaningful relationships. In some ways their behaviour is rather similar to that described for children suffering from reactive attachment disorder*.

anaclitic depression A severe form of depression identified by Spitz in infants who experienced prolonged separations from their mothers.

attachment A strong emotional tie that develops over time between an infant and its primary caregiver(s)* and results in a desire to maintain proximity.

attachment disorder *See* reactive attachment disorder.

attachment theory An account of how attachments are formed and how they promote healthy development. Bowlby presented the most well-developed theory of attachment which draws on the ideas of innate* social releasers* and an internal working model* which acts as the basis of all future relationships.

autistic, autistic disorder or autism A disorder of childhood charac- terised by socially unresponsive behaviour. Autistic children often have communication problems and engage in bizarre and stereo- typed behaviours.

behaviourism A psychological perspective which explains all behav- iour in terms of learning (conditioning) and focuses on observable events, regarding mental events as unnecessary fictions.

bond disruption When a child is deprived of their main attachment object, whether for short or long term.

bonding Forming a relationship. The term is sometimes used synony- ously with 'attachment'* but in this book has been reserved to refer to the early relationship between very young infants and their care- givers, as well as the relationship betweem some non-human young and their caregivers.*

caregiver Anyone who provides for an infant's needs, this could be parents, grandparents, siblings, day-care worker. A child may have more than one caregiver.

caregiver sensitivity hypothesis Secure attachments are due to a care- giver's sensitivity and responsiveness, which creates independence in the infant.

cognitive Of the mind – thoughts, attitudes, beliefs and so on.

collectivistic society A culture where individuals share tasks, belong- ings and income. The people may live in large family groups and value interdependence, unlike individualistic societies*.

conditioned reinforcer A thing which acts as a reinforcer because it has been associated with another reinforcer, not because it is intrinsically reinforcing. Money is an example of a conditioned reinforcer.

control group A group of participants in an experiment who receive no 'treatment' so that their behaviour can be compared with the participants who do receive 'treatment' (the experimental group). Without a control group we do not know if the experimental treat- ment did have any effect.

critical age/period A limited period during development in which a particular stimulus will have a profound effect on the organism.

The same stimulation before or after this period will have little or no effect. *See* sensitive period.

cross-cultural research An approach to research where cultures other than our own are studied and comparisons made with our own. This may be done in order (1) to identify innate* and learned behaviours, (2) to gain insights into our own cultural practices such as childrearing methods, and (3) to develop a less ethnocentric view of human behaviour.

cultural relativism The value of a behaviour or attitude can only be understood within the context of the culture in which it occurs.

culture The human-made part of the environment; the rules, morals and methods of interaction that bind a group of people and which are perpetuated through the process of socialisation.

deprivation To lose something, most importantly the care of an attachment figure. It is distinguished from privation*.

deprivation dwarfism Physical under-development found in children reared in isolation or in institutions. Thought to be an effect of the stress associated with emotional deprivation.

elaborated code A kind of language which allows a user to articulate abstract concepts more easily. Bernstein suggested it is more common in middle-class than lower-class families. *See* restricted code.

endorphins Naturally occurring opiates which are produced as a response to pain, anxiety or fear and reduce sensations of pain.

ethics The consideration of what is acceptable in human behaviour in pursuit of certain aims.

ethology The study of the whole animal, focusing on observable patterns of behaviour and their functions. It is a biological approach which, unlike psychology, does not deal with emotions or mental processes – which makes it particularly suitable for studying infants and animals who can't tell you what they feel.

evolutionary explanation An explanation based on the principles of evolution. The most important feature is the principle of natural selection – individuals (and their genes*) are selected through the natural force of the survival of the fittest. The fittest individual is the one whose characteristics promote survival and reproduction.

filial imprinting The attachment of an infant to its parent, and vice versa. It is imprinting* which results in a following response*.

fit The extent to which the demands of two individuals are in harmony. The term is also used, in evolutionary explanations, to refer to the extent that an animal's characteristics are appropriate for its environment.

following response An infant's innate* tendency to follow the individual on whom it has imprinted*.

gene A unit of inheritance which forms part of a chromosome. Some characteristics are determined by one gene whereas for others many genes are involved (polygenetic inheritance).

gene pool The whole stock of different genes in a population.

hormone A biochemical substance which profoundly affects behaviour and development. Hormones are produced in very small quantities by glands of the endocrine system. They are transported in the blood, and act rapidly but quickly disappear.

imposed etic The use of a technique developed in one culture to study another culture. The Strange Situation is one example. An 'etic' is a universal behaviour as distinct from an 'emic', which is a culturally specific behaviour.

imprint A lasting impression.

imprinting A specialised form of learning which takes place rapidly during early development and which has important consequences, such as for protection and, later, reproduction.

individualistic society A culture which emphasises individuality, individual needs and independence. People tend to live in small nuclear families unlike in collectivistic societies*.

innate Inborn, a product of genetic factors (genes*). Innate behaviours may be present at birth or may appear later as a result of maturation. The word congenital describes behaviours present at birth which are not genetic.

instinctive Behaviour which is innate* and specific to a species.

interactional synchrony The simultaneous and reciprocal influence between infant and caregiver* when interacting socially. Each individual responds to the other's social cues in harmony.

internal working model A mental model of the world which enables individuals to predict, control and manipulate their environment. Individuals have many such models, some concerned with the environment, or world in general, and others which are 'organismal' and tell us about ourselves and our relation with the world. One such organismal model is concerned with the relationship between oneself and one's primary caregiver*, and this model provides a basis for all other relationships.

IQ Intelligence quotient, a measure of intelligence. It is a score derived from an intelligence test which has been adjusted for chronological age. It is calculated by dividing mental age (test score) by chronological age and multiplying by 100. The mean IQ is 100.

kibbutz (kibbutzim) A type of Israeli farming community where most of the tasks are shared by community members, including child care. The children are all looked after in one house by metapelets*.

learned helplessness The tendency for an individual to become helpless or give up trying because previous attempts have resulted in frustration or failure.

longitudinal study A technique where research is carried out over a period of time (often years) so that changes in individuals can be observed. It is particularly used in developmental research so that the effects of independent variables on developmental outcomes can be observed.

maternal deprivation The result of the absence of a child's primary caregiver* ('mother' figure). Bowlby proposed that such absence leads to the breaking of attachment bonds and has long-term effects on emotional development (affectionless psychopathy*).

mature To develop or ripen into adulthood. Some aspects of maturation are innate*, such as the onset of puberty.

metapelet Nurse who cares for the children living on a kibbutz*.

monotropy The innate* tendency for a child to become attached to one primary caregiver*. The resulting relationship is qualitatively different from all others and has special importance for the child's internal working model* which is concerned with relationships.

nature Inherited and genetic, as distinct from nurture* which refers to all influences after conception i.e. experience.

neonate Newborn.

nurture The influence of experience as distinct from nature*.

object permanence A feature of the sensorimotor stage* in cognitive* development. Described by Piaget as a time at which an infant understands that when objects are hidden from view they still continue to exist. Piaget suggested that this occurs around the age of 8 months though other research has found evidence that babies may be aware of object permanence at a much earlier age.

oral deprivation A Freudian concept to describe the effects of deprivation during the oral stage* of infant development.

oral stage The first psychosexual stage of infant development, during which the infant seeks and derives pleasure from oral satisfaction.

PDD model Protest–despair–detachment, the model of separation anxiety first described by Bowlby and Robertson.

precocial Animals who are mobile from birth, as distinct from altricial species.

prenatal Before birth.

primary emotions The emotions which are universal and innate*, such as fear, anger, sadness, joy and disgust. *See* secondary emotions.

privation A term introduced by Rutter to describe the lack of any attachments as distinct from the loss of attachments (deprivation*).

psychoanalysis The Freudian theories of personality development and the therapy derived from it.

reactive attachment disorder A condition where children lack the ability to give and receive affection. Symptoms include cruelty to others especially pets, abnormalities in eye contact and speech patterns, lying and stealing, lack of long-term friends, and extreme control problems. The diagnosis is only made when there are no other likely causes for the lack of social responsiveness, such as mental retardation.

readiness The state of being ready to benefit from a particular experience as a result of maturation.

reinforcement The process by which a response is strengthened or made more likely in the future. Positive reinforcement occurs when a response is followed by something pleasant, negative reinforcement occurs when a response is followed by the removal of something unpleasant.

reordered families Families where the parents have divorced, remarried and taken on stepfamilies.

restricted code A kind of language which restricts cognitive* development because it lacks the ability to easily express abstract concepts. *See* elaborated code.

schema An organised packet of information or data structure which contains knowledge. It acts like an internal working model* in organising past experiences and generating expectations for future ones. We have schema for everything, from how to give a birthday party to the concept of a tree.

secondary emotions Emotions which are learned and culturally specific. *See* primary emotions.

secure base A way to describe the role of an attachment figure as a starting point from which to explore and learn about the world.

sensitive period A period of time during which an individual is best able to learn a particular response. The individual can learn the same thing at other ages but not as rapidly or easily. It is generally preferred to the concept of a critical period*.

sensorimotor stage Piaget's first stage of cognitive* development which occurs between the ages of 0 to 2 years. The infant learns to coordinate its motor and sensory systems through circular (repetitive) actions and to form schemas.*

separation anxiety The sense of concern felt by a child when separated from his/her attachment figure. The infant becomes progressively more anxious as described by the PDD model*.

separation protest The infant's behaviour when separated – crying or holding out their arms. Some insecurely attached infants show no protest when left by their attachment figure, whereas securely attached children do.

SES Socioeconomic status. The social position held by an individual as defined in terms of family background, social class, education of parents and self, values and so on.

sexual imprinting A form of imprinting* by which an individual learns to identify members of its own species and used later as the basis for selecting sexual partners.

sociability The tendency to seek and enjoy the company of others. It is an innate* temperamental* characteristic which is then reinforced by experience.

social referencing Using the behaviour of others as a guide for social behaviour.

social releaser A social behaviour or characteristic which, among other things, elicits a caregiving reaction. Bowlby suggested that these were innate* and critical in the process of forming attachments*.

stage theories A theory of development where different stages are identified. The key feature is that the stages occur in a fixed sequence and at (approximately) predictable ages.

Strange Situation An experimental procedure used to test the security of a child's attachment to a caregiver. The key features are what the child does when it is left by the caregiver* and the child's behaviour at reunion, as well as responses to a stranger.

stranger anxiety The distress experienced by a child when approached by a stranger. Children first show this in the second half of their first year.

supra-individual Above the level of the individual. The term is used to describe the fact that animals have an innate* predisposition to imprint* on a class of objects (for example, things which move or make a particular sound) rather than any individual.

temperament A person's characteristic modes of emotional response, such as sociability. Such tendencies are to some extent innate* and subsequently modified by experience

theory of mind Our understanding that other people have separate mental states and see the world from their point of view which differs from our own. Young children do not have this theory of mind and can't imagine that someone else is experiencing different feelings or thoughts.

verbal deprivation theory Bernstein's theory that restricted code* (language) limits cognitive* development.

References

Ahrens, R. (1954) Beitrag zur Entwicklung des Physiognomie und Minierkenntnis. *Zeitschrift für Experimentelle und Angewandte Psychologie*, 2, 412–454.

Ainsworth, M.D.S. (1967) *Infancy in Uganda: child care and the growth of love*. Baltimore: Johns Hopkins University Press.

—— (1972) The effects of maternal deprivation: a review of findings and controversy in the context of research strategy. In *Deprivation of maternal care: a reassessment of its effects*, World Health Organisation, Geneva.

—— (1973) The development of mother-infant attachment. In B.M. Caldwell and H.N. Ricciutti (eds), *Review of child development research* (Vol. 3). Chicago: University of Chicago Press.

—— (1979) Attachment as related to mother–infant interaction. In J.G. Rosenblatt, R.A. Hinde, C. Beer and M. Busnel (eds), *Advances in the study of behaviour* (Vol. 9). Orlando, FL: Academic Press.

—— (1982) Attachment: retrospect and prospect. In C.M. Parkes and J. Stevenson-Hinde (eds), *The place of attachment in behaviour*. London: Tavistock.

—— (1989) Attachments beyond infancy. *American Psychologist*, 44, 709–716.

Ainsworth, M.D.S., Bell, S.M. and Stayton, D.J. (1974) Infant/mother attachment and social development as a product of reciprocal responsiveness to signals. In M.P.M. Richards (ed.), *The integration of the child into a social world*. Cambridge: Cambridge University Press.

Ainsworth, M.D.S., Blehar, M.C., Waters, E. and Wall, S. (1978) *Patterns of attachment: a psychological study of the strange situation*. Hillsdale, NJ: Lawrence Erlbaum.

Alley, T.R. (1981) Head shape and the perception of cuteness. *Developmental Psychology*, 17, 650–654.

Amato, P.R. (1993) Children's adjustment to divorce: theories, hypotheses, and empirical support. *Journal of Marriage and the Family*, 55, 23–38.

Amato, P.R., Loomis, L.S. and Booth, A. (1995) Parental divorce, marital conflict, and offspring well-being during early adulthood. *Social Forces*, 73 (3), 895–915.

Ambrose, J.A. (1961) The development of the smiling response in early infancy. In B.M. Foss (ed.), *Determinants of infant behaviour* (Vol. 1). London: Methuen.

Anderson, J. (1972) Attachment out of doors. In N. Blurton-Jones (ed.), *Ethological studies of child behaviour*. Cambridge: Cambridge University Press.

Andersson, B.E. (1996) Children's development related to day-care, type of family and other home factors. *European Child and Adolescent Psychiatry*, 5 (1), 73–75.

Banks, M.S., Aslin, R.N. and Weiskopf, S. (1975) Sensitive period for the development of human binocular vision. *Science*, 190, 675–677.

Baron-Cohen, S., Leslie, A.M. and Frith, U. (1985) Does the autistic child have a 'theory of mind'? *Cognition*, 21, 37–46.

Barrett, H. (1997) How young children cope with separation: toward a new conceptualization. *British Journal of Medical Psychology*, 70, 339–358.

Barry, H., Bacon, M.K. and Child, I.L. (1957) A cross-cultural survey of some sex differences in socialisation. *Journal of Abnormal and Social Psychology*, 55, 327–332.

Baumrind, D. (1971) Current patterns of parental authority. *Developmental Psychology Monographs*, 4 (1,2).

Bee, H. (1995) *The developing child* (7th edition). New York: HarperCollins.

Bell, S.M. and Ainsworth, M.D.S. (1972) Infant crying and maternal responsiveness. *Child Development*, 43 (4), 1,171–1,190.

Benton, D. and Cook, R. (1991) Vitamin and mineral supplements improve intelligence scores and concentration. *Personality and Individual Differences*, 12 (11), 1,151–1,158.

Bernstein, B. (1961) Social class and linguistic development. In A.H. Halsey, J. Flaud and C.A. Anderson (eds), *Education, economy and society*. London: Collier-Macmillan Ltd.

Blakemore, C. and Cooper, G.F. (1970) Development of the brain depends on visual environment. *Nature*, 228, 477–478.

Bohman, M. and Sigvardsson, S. (1979) Long-term effects of early institutional care: a prospective longitudinal study. *Annual Progress in Child Psychiatry and Child Development*, 148–156.

Bowlby, J. (1944) Forty-four juvenile thieves: their characters and their home life. *International Journal of Psychoanalysis*, 25, 1–57, 207–228.

—— (1946) *Forty-four juvenile thieves*. London: Balliére, Tindall and Cox.

—— (1951) *Maternal care and mental health*. Geneva: World Health Organisation.

—— (1953) *Child care and the growth of love*. Harmondsworth: Penguin.

—— (1961) Processes of mourning. *International Journal of Psychoanalysis*, 41 (2–3), 317–340.

—— (1969) *Attachment and loss. Vol. 1: Attachment*. London: Hogarth Press.

—— (1973) *Attachment and loss. Vol. 2: Separation, anxiety and anger*. London: Hogarth Press.

—— (1980) *Attachment and loss. Vol. 3: Loss, sadness and depression*. London: Hogarth Press.

—— (1988) *A secure base: clinical applications of attachment theory*. London: Routledge.

Bowlby, J., Ainsworth, M., Boston, M. and Rosenbluth, D. (1956) The effects of mother–child separation: a follow-up study. *British Journal of Medical Psychology*, 29, 211.

Bowlby, J., Robertson, J. and Rosenbluth, J. (1952) A two-year-old goes to hospital. *The Psychoanalytic Study of the Child*, 7, 82–94.

Bradley, L. and Bryant, P.E. (1983) Categorizing sounds and learning to read: a causal connection. *Nature*, 301, 419–421.

Brazelton, T.B., Tronick, E., Adamson, L., Als, H. and Wise, S. (1975) Early mother–infant reciprocity. *Parent–Infant Interaction Ciba Foundation Symposium*, 33, 137–154.

Brody, V.A. (1978) A developmental play: a relationship-focused program for children. *Child Welfare*, 57 (9), 591–599.

Bryant, B., Harris, M. and Newton, D. (1980) *Children and minders*. London: Grant McIntyre.

Bryant, P.E. and Bradley, L. (1985) *Children's reading problems*. Oxford: Basil Blackwell.

Bus, A.G. and Van IJzendoorn, M.H. (1988) Attachment and early reading: a longitudinal study. *Journal of Genetic Psychology*, 149 (2), 199–210.

Bushnell, I., Sai, F. and Mullin, J.T. (1989) Neonatal recognition of the mother's face. *British Journal of Developmental Psychology*, 7, 3–15.

Campos, J., Barrett, K., Lamb, M., Goldsmith, H. and Sternberg, C. (1983) Socioemotional development. In M. Haith and J. Campos (eds), *Infancy and developmental psychobiology*. Vol. 2 of P. Mussen, *Handbook of Child Psychology*. New York: Wiley.

Cardwell, M. (1996) *The complete A–Z psychology handbook*. London: Hodder and Stoughton.

Cernoch, J.M. and Porter, R.H. (1985) Recognition of maternal axillary odours by infants. *Child Development*, 56, 1,593–1,598.

Chess, S., Thomas, A., Mittleman, M., Korn, S. and Cohen, J. (1984) Early parental attitudes, divorce and separation, and young adult outcome: findings of a longitudinal study. *Annual Progress in Child Psychiatry and Child Development*, 281–289.

Clarke, A.D.B. and Clarke, A.M. (1979) Early experience: its limited effect upon later development. In D. Shaffer and J. Dunn (eds), *The first year of life*. Chichester: John Wiley.

Clarke, A.M. and Clarke, A.D.B. (1976) *Early experience: myth and evidence*. New York: Free Press.

—— (1998) Early experience and the life path. *The Psychologist*, 11 (9), 433–436.

Clarke-Stewart, K.A., Gruber, C.P. and Fitzgerald, L.M. (1994) *Children at home and in day care*. Hillsdale, NJ: Erlbaum.

Cockett, M. and Tripp, J. (1994) Children living in disordered families. *Social Policy Research Findings*, no. 45. Joseph Rowntree Foundation.

Curtiss, S. (1977) *Genie: a psycholinguistic study of a modern-day 'wild child'*. London: Academic Press.

Das, J.P. (1973) Helping strategies for disadvantaged children. *Mental Retardation Bulletin*, 2 (1), 4–8.

Davenport, G.C. (1991) *An introduction to child development*. London: Collins Educational.

Davis, K. (1947) Final note on a case of extreme isolation. *American Journal of Sociology*, 52, 432–437.

De Chateau, P. and Wiberg, B. (1977) Long-term effect on mother–infant behavior of extra contact during the first hour post-partum. I. First observation at 36 hours. *Acta Paediatrica Scandinavica*, 66, 137–144.

Dennis, W. (1960) Causes of retardation amongst institutional children: Iran. *Journal of Genetic Psychology*, 96, 47–59.

Douglas, J.W.B. (1975) Early hospital admissions and later disturbances of behaviour and learning. *Developmental Medical Child Neurology, 17*, 456–480.

Dunn, J., Plomin, R. and Daniels, D. (1986) Consistency and change in mothers' behaviour towards young siblings. *Child Development*, 57, 348–356.

Erickson, M.F., Sroufe, L.A. and Egeland, B. (1985) The relationship between quality of attachment and behaviour problems in preschool in a high-risk sample. *Monographs for the Society for Research in Child Development*, 50 (1–2), 147–166.

Erikson, E.H. (1963) *Childhood and society* (2nd edition). New York: Norton.

Fantz, R.L. (1961) The origin of form perception. *Scientific American*, 204 (5), 66–72.

Feldman, D.H. (1986) *Nature's gambit: child prodigies and the development of human potential*. New York: Basic Books.

Field, T. (1978) Interaction behaviours of primary versus secondary caretaker fathers. *Developmental Psychology*, 14, 183–184.

Flanagan, C. (1996) *Applying psychology to early child development*. London: Hodder and Stoughton.

Fowler, W. (1990) Early stimulation and the development of verbal talents. In M.J.A. Howe (ed.), *Encouraging the development of exceptional abilities and talents.* Leicester: BPS Books.

Fox, N. (1977) Attachment of kibbutz infants to mother and metapelet. *Child Development,* 48, 1,228–1,239.

Freeman, N.H. (1974) *Human infancy: an evolutionary perspective.* Hillsdale, NJ: Erlbaum.

Freud, A. and Dann, S. (1951) An experiment in group upbringing. *Psychoanalytic Study of the Child,* 6, 127–168.

Furman, W., Rahe, D.F. and Hartup, W.W. (1979) Rehabilitation of socially withdrawn preschool children through mixed-age and same-age socialisation. *Child Development,* 50, 915–922.

Garland, C. and White, S. (1980) *Children and day nurseries.* London: Grant McIntyre.

Gibson, E.J., Gibson, J.J., Pick, A.D. and Osser, H.A. (1962) A developmental study of the discrimination of letter-like forms. *Journal of Comparative and Physiological Psychology,* 55, 897–906.

Gilhousen, M.R., Allen, L.F. Lasater, L.M., Farrell, D.M. *et al.* (1990) Veracity and vicissitude: A critical look at the Milwaukee Project. *Journal of School Psychology,* 28 (4), 285–299.

Goldberg, S. (1983) Parent–infant bonding: another look. *Child Development,* 54, 1,355–1,382.

Goldsmith, H.H., Buss, A.H., Plomin, R., Rothbart, M.K., Thomas, A., Chess, S., Hinde, R.A. and McCall, R.B. (1987) Roundtable: What is temperament? Four approaches. *Child Development,* 58, 505–529.

Goren, C.C., Sarty, M. and Wu, P.Y.K. (1975) Visual following and pattern discrimination of face-like stimuli by newborn infants. *Pediatrics,* 56, 544–549.

Grossmann, K.E. and Grossmann, K. (1991) Attachment quality as an organizer of emotional and behavioural responses in a longitudinal perspective. In C.M. Parkes, J. Stevenson-Hinde and P. Marris (eds), *Attachment across the life cycle.* London: Tavistock/Routledge.

Guiton, P. (1966) Early experience and sexual object choice in the brown leghorn. *Animal Behaviour,* 14, 534–538.

Harkness, S. and Super, C.M. (1992) Parental ethnotheories in action. In I.E. Siegel (ed.), *Parental belief systems: the psychological consequences for children.* Hillsdale, NJ: Erlbaum.

Harlow, H.F. (1949) Formation of learning sets. *Psychological Review*, 56, 51–65.

—— (1958) The nature of love. *American Psychologist*, 13, 673–685.

—— (1959) Love in infant monkeys. *Scientific American*, 200 (6), 68–74.

Harlow, H.F. and Harlow, M.K. (1962) Social deprivation in monkeys. *Scientific American*, 207 (5), 136–146.

Harlow, H.F. and Zimmerman, R.R. (1959) Affectional responses in the infant monkey. *Science*, 130, 421–432.

Haskins, R. (1989) Beyond metaphor: the efficacy of early childhood education. *American Psychologist*, 44, 274–282.

Hazan, C. and Shaver, P.R. (1987) Romantic love conceptualised as an attachment process. *Journal of Personality and Social Psychology*, 52, 511–524.

Hazen, N.L. and Durrett, M.E. (1982) Relationship of security of attachment to exploration and cognitive mapping abilities in 2-year-olds. *Developmental Psychology*, 18, 751–759.

Heber, R., Garber, H., Harrington, S., Hoffman, C. and Falender, C. (1972) *Rehabilitation of families at risk for mental retardation: progress report*. University of Wisconsin: Rehabilitation Research and Training Centre in Mental Retardation.

Herrnstein, R.J. and Murray, C. (1994) *The Bell Curve: intelligence and class structure in American life*. New York: Free Press.

Hess, E.H. (1958) Imprinting in animals. *Scientific American*, 198, 81–90.

Hinde, R.A. (1982) Attachment: some conceptual and biological issues. In C.M. Parkes and J. Stevenson-Hinde (eds), *The place of attachment in behaviour*. London: Tavistock.

—— (1982) *Ethology*. Oxford: Oxford University Press and London: Fontana Paperback.

—— (1987) *Individuals, relationships and culture: links between ethology and the social sciences*. Cambridge: Cambridge University Press.

Hinde, R.A. and Stevenson-Hinde, J. (1976) Towards understanding relationships: dynamic stability. In P.P.G. Bateson and R.A. Hinde (eds), *Growing points in ethology*. Cambridge: Cambridge University Press.

Hodges, J. and Tizard, B. (1989) Social and family relationships of ex-institutional adolescents. *Journal of Child Psychology and Psychiatry*, 30 (1), 77–97.

Hoffman, H.S. (1996) *Amorous turkeys and addicted ducklings: a search for the causes of social attachment*. Boston, MA: Author's Cooperative.

Hoffman, M.L. (1970) Moral development. In P.H. Mussen (ed.), *Carmichael's manual of child psychology* (Vol. 2). New York: Wiley.

Hogg, M.P., Nadler, R.D., Hoff, K.T. and Maple, T.L. (1994) Separation and depression in infant gorillas. *Developmental Psychobiology*, 27 (7), 439–452.

Holmes, J. (1993) *John Bowlby and Attachment Theory*. London: Routledge.

Howe, M.J.A. (1990) *Sense and nonsense about hothouse children*. BPS Books.

—— (1995) Hothouse tots. *Psychology Review*, 2 (1), 2–4.

—— (1998) Intelligence: some questions answered. *Psychology Review*, 5 (1), 2–5.

Howes, C. and Hamilton, C.E. (1992) Children's relationships with caregivers: mothers and child care teachers. *Child Development*, 63 (4), 859–866.

Howes, C., Galinsky, E. and Kontos, S. (1998) Child care: caregiver sensitivity and attachment. *Social Development*, 7 (1), 25–36.

Howes, C., Matheson, C.C. and Hamilton, C.E. (1994) Maternal, teacher, and child care correlates of children's relationships with peers. *Child Development*, 65 (1), 264–273.

Immelmann, K. (1972) Sexual and other long-term aspects of imprinting in birds and other species. In D.S. Lehrmann, R.A. Hinde and E. Shaw (eds), *Advances in the study of behaviour* (Vol. 4). New York: Academic Press.

Izard, C.E. (1982) *Measuring emotions in infants and children*. New York: Cambridge University Press.

Izard, C.E., Huebner, R.R., Risser, D., McGinnies, G. and Dougherty, L. (1980) The young infant's ability to produce discrete emotion expressions. *Developmental Psychology*, 16, 132–140.

Jacobson, J.L. and Wille, D.E. (1986) The influence of attachment pattern on developmental changes in peer interaction from the toddler to the preschool period. *Child Development*, 57, 338–347.

Johnson, W., Emde, R.N., Pannabecker, B., Stenberg, C. and Davis, M. (1982) Maternal perception of infant emotion from birth through to 18 months. *Infant Behaviour and Development*, 5, 313–322.

Jones, D.N., Pickett, J., Oates, M.R. and Barbor, P. (1987) *Understanding child abuse* (2nd edition). London: Macmillan.

Kagan, J. and Klein, R.E. (1973) Cross-cultural perspectives on early development. *American Psychologist*, 28, 947–961.

Kagan, J., Kearsley, R.B. and Zelazo, P.R. (1980) *Infancy: its place in human development*. Cambridge, MA: Harvard University Press.

Kiecolt-Glaser, J.K., Garner, W., Speicher, C.E., Penn, G.M., Holliday, J. and Glaser, R. (1984) Psychosocial modifiers of immunocompetence in medical students. *Psychosomatic Medicine*, 46, 7–14.

Kirkby, R.J. and Whelan, R.J. (1996) The effects of hospitalisation and medical procedures on children and their families. *Journal of Family Studies*, 2 (1), 65–77.

Klaus, M.H. and Kennell, J.H. (1976) *Maternal–infant bonding*. St Louis: Mosby.

—— (1982) *Parent–infant bonding*. St Louis: Mosby.

Koluchová, J. (1972) Severe deprivation in twins: a case study. *Journal of Child Psychology and Psychiatry*, 13, 107–114.

—— (1976) The further development of twins after severe and prolonged deprivation: a second report. *Journal of Child Psychology and Psychiatry*, 17, 181–188.

—— (1991) Severely deprived twins after twenty-two years' observation. *Studia Psychologica*, 33, 23–28.

Konner, M.J. (1981) Evolution of human behaviour development. In R.H. Munroe, R.L. Munroe and B.B. Whiting (eds), *Handbook of cross-cultural human development*. New York: Garland.

Kunkel, J.H. (1985) Vivaldi in Venice: an historical test of psychological propositions. *Psychological Record, 35*, 445–457.

Labov, W. (1969) The logic of nonstandard English. In P.P. Giglioli (ed.), *Language and social context*. Harmondsworth, Middlesex: Penguin.

—— (1970) The logic of non-standard English. In F. Williams (ed.), *Language and poverty*. Chicago: Markham.

Lamb, M.E. (1981) The development of father–infant relationships. In M.E. Lamb (ed.), *The role of the father in child development*. New York: Wiley.

Lamb, M.E., Thompson, R.A., Gardner, W.P., Charnov, E.L. and Estes, D. (1984) Security of infantile attachment as assessed in the strange situation: Its study and biological interpretation. *Brain and Behavioral Sciences*, 7, 127–147.

Lazar, I. and Darlington, R. (1982) Lasting effects of early education: a report from the Consortium for Longitudinal Studies. *Monographs of the Society for Research in Child Development*, 47, nos. 2–3.

Logan , B. (1987) Teaching the unborn: precept and practice. *Pre- and Peri-Natal Psychology Journal*, 2 (1), 9–24.

Lorenz, K. (1935) Der Kumpan in der Umwelt des Vogels. *Journal of Ornithology*, 83, 137–213. Published in English, Lorenz (1937).

—— (1937) The companion in the bird's world. *Auk*, 54, 245–273.

—— (1943) The innate forms of possible experience. *Zeitschrift für Tierpsychologie*, 5, 233–409.

—— (1952) *King Solomon's Ring: new light on animal ways*. London: Methuen and Co.

—— (1958) The evolution of behaviour. *Scientific American*, 199 (6), 67–78.

—— (1966) *On aggression*. New York: Harcourt, Brace and World.

Lynch, M. and Roberts, J. (1982) *Consequences of child abuse*. London: Academic Press.

Lynn, R. (1986) The rise of national intelligence: the evidence from Britain, Japan and the USA. *Personality and Individual Differences*, 7 (1), 23–32.

Maccoby, E.E. (1980) *Social development: psychological growth and the parent–child relationship*. San Diego: Harcourt Brace Jovanovich.

MacDonald, K. and Parke, R.D. (1984) Bridging the gap: parent–child play interaction and peer interactive competence. *Child Development*, 55, 1,265–1,277.

Main, M. and Solomon, J. (1986) Discovery of a disorganized/disoriented attachment pattern. In T.B. Brazelton and M.W. Yogman (eds), *Affective development in infancy*. Norwood, NJ: Ablex.

Main, M. and Weston, D.R. (1981) The quality of the toddler's relationship to mother and father related to conflict and the readiness to establish new relationships. *Child Development*, 52, 932–940.

Main, M., Kaplan, N. and Cassidy, J. (1985) Security in infancy: a move to a level of representation. In I. Bretherton and E. Waters (eds), *Growing points of attachment theory and research*. Monographs of the Society for Research in Child Development, 50 (1–2), Serial no. 209.

Marler, P. and Mundinger, P. (1971) Vocal learning in birds. In H. Moltz (ed.), *The ontogeny of vertebrate behaviour*. New York: Academic Press.

Mason, M.K. (1942) Learning to speak after six and one-half years silence. *Journal of Speech Disorders*, 7, 295–304.

Matheny, A.P. (1983) A longitudinal twin study of the stability of components from Bayley's Infant Behaviour Record. *Child Development*, 54, 356–360.

Maurer, D. and Maurer C. (1989) *The world of the newborn*. Viking.

Mayall, B. and Petrie, P. (1983) *Childminding and day nurseries: what kind of care?* London: Heinemann Educational Books.

Mead, M. (1935) *Sex and temperament in three primitive societies*. New York: Morrow.

Meltzoff, A. and Moore, M. (1983) New born infants imitate adult facial gestures. *Child Development*, 54, 702–709.

—— (1989) Imitation in newborn infants: exploring the range of gestures initiated and the underlying mechanisms. *Developmental Psychology*, 25, 954–962.

—— (1977) Imitation of facial and manual gestures by human neonates. *Science*, 198, 75–78.

—— (1992) Early imitation within a functional framework: the importance of person identity, movement and development. *Infant Behaviour and Development*, 15 (4), 479–505.

Minturn, L. and Lambert, W.W. (1964) *Mothers of six cultures*. New York: Wiley.

Mizuta, I., Zahn-Wexler, C. and Hiruma, N. (1996) A cross-cultural study of preschoolers' attachment: security and sensitivity in Japanese and US dyads. *International Journal of Behavioural Development*, 19 (1), 141–159.

Morison, S.J., Ames, E.W. and Chisholm, K. (1995) The development of children adopted from Romanian orphanages. *Merrill Palmer Quarterly*, 41 (4), 411–430.

Munroe, R.H. and Munroe, R.L. (1980) Infant experience and childhood affect among the Logoli: a longitudinal study. *Ethos*, 8 (4), 295–315.

Myers, B.J. (1984) Mother–infant bonding: the status of this critical period hypothesis. *Developmental Review*, 4, 240–274.

Nakagawa, M., Lamb, M.E. and Miyaki, K. (1992) Antecedents and correlates of the Strange Situation behavior of Japanese infants. *Journal of Cross-Cultural Psychology*, 23 (3), 300–310.

Novak, M.A. and Harlow, H.F. (1975) Social recovery of monkeys isolated for the first years of life. I: Rehabilitation and therapy. *Developmental Psychology*, 11, 453–465.

Oden, S. and Asher, S.R. (1977) Coaching children in social skills for friendship making. *Child Development*, 48, 495–506.

Papousek, H. and Papousek, M. (1975) Cognitive aspects of preverbal social infant–adult interaction. *Parent–Infant Interaction*: Ciba Foundation Symposium, 33, 240–259.

Parke, R.D. (1981) *Fathers*. Cambridge, MA: Harvard University Press.

Parker, K.C. and Forrest, D. (1993) Attachment disorder: an emerging concern for school counselors. *Elementary School Guidance and Counseling*, 27 (3), 209–215.

Piaget, J. (1970) Piaget's theory. In P.H. Mussen (ed.) *Carmichael's manual of child psychology,* (Vol. 1) New York: Wiley.

Portnoy, S., Halpern, P.D. and Lindblad, M. (1973) A comprehensive cognitively and affectively enriched summer day camp for inner-city children. *Proceedings of the Annual Convention of the American Psychological Association*, 959–960.

Pringle, M.L.K. and Bossio, V. (1960) Early prolonged separations and emotional adjustment. *Journal of Child Psychology and Psychiatry*, 1, 37–48.

Quinton, D. and Rutter, M. (1976) Early hospital admissions and later disturbance of behaviour: an attempted replication of Douglas's findings. *Developmental Medicine and Child Neurology*, 18, 447–459.

—— (1988) *Parental breakdown: the making and breaking of intergenerational links*. Gower.

Ramey, C.T. (1993) A rejoinder to Spitz's critique of the Abecedarian experiment. *Intelligence*, 17, 25–30.

Reber, A.S. (1995) *The Penguin Dictionary of Psychology*. Harmondsworth, Middlesex: Penguin.

Rheingold, H.L. and Eckerman, C.D. (1970) The infant separates himself from his mother. *Science*, 168, 78–83.

Robertson, J. (1952) *A two-year-old goes to hospital* (Film). London: Tavistock Child Development Research Unit.

Robertson, J. and Bowlby, J. (1952) Responses of young children to separation from their mothers. *Courier Centre International de l'Enfance*, 2 (3), 131–142.

Robertson, J. and Robertson, J. (1967–73) *Young children in brief separation* (Film). London: Tavistock Child Development Research Unit.

—— (1968) Young children in brief separation: a fresh look. *Psychoanalytic Study of the Child*, 26, 264–315.

Rodman, D. (1987) *The spontaneous gesture*. Cambridge, MA: Harvard University Press.

Rogers, C.R. (1961) *On becoming a person*. Boston: Houghton Mifflin.

Roopnarine, J.L. and Lamb, M.E. (1980) The effects of day care on attachment and exploratory behavior in a strange situation. *Advances in Family Psychiatry*, 2, 469–479.

Rosenblum, L.A. and Harlow, H.F. (1963) Approach-avoidance conflict in the mother surrogate situation. *Psychological Reports*, 12, 83–85.

Rosenhan, D.L. (1970) The natural socialisation of altruistic autonomy. In J.L. Macaulay and L. Berkowitz (eds), *Altruism and helping behaviour*. New York: Academic Press.

Rutter, M. (1972) *Maternal deprivation reassessed* (1st edition). Harmondsworth, Middlesex: Penguin.

—— (1981) *Maternal deprivation reassessed* (2nd edition). Harmondsworth, Middlesex: Penguin.

Rutter, M. *et al.* (1998) Developmental catch-up and deficit, following adoption after severe global early privation. *Journal of Child Psychology and Psychiatry*, 39, 465–476.

Rymer, R. (1993) *Genie: Escape from a silent childhood*. London: Michael Joseph.

Scarr, S. (1968) Environmental bias in twin studies *Eugenics Quarterly*, 15, 34–40.

Schaffer, H.R. (1974) Cognitive components of the infants response to strangeness. In M. Lewis and L. Rosenblum: *The origins of fear*. New York: Wiley.

—— (1996) *Social development*. Oxford: Blackwell.

—— (1998) Cross-cultural perspectives on child development. *Psychology Review*, 4 (3), 2–6.

Schaffer, H.R. and Emerson, P.E. (1964) The development of social attachments in infancy. *Monographs of the Society for Research in Child Development*, 29 (3 Serial No. 94).

Schwartz, G., Weinberger, C. and Singer, J. (1981) Cardiovascular differentiation of happiness, sadness, anger and fear following imagery and exercise. *Psychosomatic Medicine*, 43, 343–364.

Schwartz, S., Deutsch, C.P. and Weissmann, A. (1967) Language development in two groups of socially disadvantaged young children. *Psychological Reports*, 21 (1), 169–178.

Seitz, V. (1990) Intervention programs for impoverished children: a comparison of educational and family support models. *Annals of Child Development: A research annual*, 7, 73–103.

Seligman, M.E.P. (1975) *Helplessness: on depression, development and death*. San Francisco: W.H. Freeman.

Shaffer, D.R. (1993) *Developmental psychology: childhood and adolescence* (3rd edition). Pacific Grove, CA: Brooks/Cole Publishing Co.

Shepher, J. (1971) Mate selection among second generation kibbutz adolescents and adults. *Archives of Sexual Behaviour*, 1, 293–307.

Sinclair-de-Zwart, H. (1969) Developmental psycholinguistics. In D. Elkind and J. Flavell (eds), *Studies in cognitive development*. New York: Oxford University Press.

Skeels, H. and Dye, H.B. (1939) A study of the effects of differential stimulation on mentally retarded children. *Proceedings and Addresses of the American Association on Mental Deficiency*, 44, 114–136.

Skeels, H. (1966) Adult status of children with contrasting early life experiences: a follow-up study. *Monographs of Society for Research of Child Development*, 31 (3) whole issue.

Skodak, M. and Skeels, H. (1949) A final follow-up study of 100 adopted children. *Journal of Genetic Psychology*, 75, 85–125.

—— (1945) A follow-up study of children in adoptive homes. *Journal of Genetic Psychology*, 66, 21–58.

Slater, A. (1990) Infant development: the origins of competence. *The Psychologist*, 3(3), 109–113.

Sluckin, W. (1965) *Imprinting and early experiences*. London: Methuen.

Spitz , R.A. (1945) Hospitalism: an inquiry into the genesis of psychiatric conditions in early childhood. In A. Freud (ed.), *The psychoanalytic study of the child* (Vol. 1). New York: International Universities Press.

Spitz, R.A. and Wolf, K.M. (1946) Anaclitic depression. *Psychoanalytic Study of the Child*, 2, 313–342.

Sroufe, L.A. (1985) Attachment classification from the perspective of infant–caregiver relationships and infant temperament. *Child Development*, 56, 1–14.

Stern, D. (1977) *The first relationship: infant and mother*. London: Open Books.

Suomi, S.J. (1976) Factors affecting responses to social separation in rhesus monkeys. In G. Serban and A. Kling (eds), *Animal models in human psychobiology*.

Takahaski, K. (1990) Are the key assumptions of the Strange Situation procedure universal? A view from Japanese research. *Human development*, 33, 23–30.

Thomas, A. and Chess, S. (1977) *Temperament and development*. New York: Brunner/Mazel.

Thomas, L.K. (1998) Multicultural aspects of attachment. http://www.bereavement.demon.co.uk/lbn/attachment/lennox/html. See also Thomas, L.K. (1995) Psychotherapy in the context of race and culture. In S. Fernando (ed.), *Mental health in a multi-ethnic society*. London: Routledge.

Tizard, B. (1979) Language at home and at school. In C.B. Cazden and D. Harvey (eds), *Language in early childhood education*. Washington, DC: National Association for the Education of Young Children.

Tizard , B. and Hodges, J. (1978) The effect of early institutional rearing on the development of eight-year-old children. *Journal of Child Psychology and Psychiatry*, 19, 99–118.

Tizard, B. and Rees, J. (1975) A comparison of the effects of adoption, restoration to the natural mother, and continued institutionalisation on the cognitive development of 4-year-old children. *Child Development*, 45, 92–99.

Trevarthan, C. (1979) Communication and cooperation in early infancy: a description of primary intersubjectivity. In M. Bullowa (ed.), *Before speech: the beginning of interpersonal communication*. Cambridge: Cambridge University Press.

Triseliotis, J. (1984) Identity and security in adoption and long-term fostering. *Early Child Development and Care*, 15 (2–3), 149–170.

Tronick, E.Z. (1989) Emotions and emotional communication in infants. *American Psychologist*, 44, 112–119.

Tronick, E.Z., Morelli, G.A. and Ivey, P.K. (1992) The Efe forager infant and toddler's pattern of social relationships: multiple and simultaneous. *Developmental Psychology*, 28, 568–577.

Turnbull, C. (1972) *The mountain people*. New York: Simon and Schuster.

Van IJzendoorn, M. and Kroonenberg, P. (1988) Cross-cultural patterns of attachment: a meta-analysis of the Strange Situation. *Child Development*, 59, 147–156.

Wallerstein, J. and Kelly, J. (1985) *Surviving the breakup*. London: Grant McIntyre.

Waters, E. (1978) The reliability and stability of individual differences in infant-mother attachment. *Child Development*, 49, 483–494.

Watson, J.B. (1928) *Psychological care of infant and child*. New York: Norton.

Westermarck, E. (1891) *The history of human marriage*. London: Macmillan.

White, B.L. and Held, R. (1966) Plasticity of sensorimotor development. In J.F. Rosenblith and W. Allensmith (eds), *The causes of behaviour* (2nd edition). Boston: Allyn and Bacon.

Whiting, B.B. (1963) *Six cultures: studies in child rearing*. New York: Wiley.

Whiting, B.B. and Whiting, J.W.M. (1975) *Children of six cultures*. Cambridge, MA: Harvard University Press.

Widdowson, E.M. (1951) Mental contentment and physical growth. *Lancet*, 1, 1,316–1,318.

Zigler, E. and Muenchow, S. (1992) Head Start: the inside story of America's most successful educational experiment. New York: Basic Books.

Index